PREFACE.

PAPER is now become the grand currency in commercial dealings, and an ample substitute for cash; insomuch that it has almost superseded the circulation of specie. We are convinced of the propriety of what has been asserted by a certain exalted character, "That we eat and drink paper, and live upon paper." It is therefore essentially necessary for us to be acquainted with the laws, by which that substitute or medium for money is to be regulated.

Bills of Exchange, Promissory Notes, Bank-Notes, Bankers' Notes, Drafts, and Checks, being, to many purposes, considered as Money; a code of Law, and the custom of merchants, respecting their regulation and proper use, seems highly necessary; and more particularly so, as there are a great number of modern decisions on certain points, which are absolutely requisite, from time to time, to be introduced into that code. New difficulties on this subject are continually starting for discussion and decision; the result of which it is important to register or record, that recourse may at all times be had to such a fountain of intelligence.

Besides

Befides the Statutes and Reports which have been promulgated upon thefe fubjects, we have confulted all the modern Treatifes that we fuppofed might probably afford us any ufeful hints relative to thefe fubftitutes for fpecie; and we acknowledge to have enriched our performance by fome of their communications. Our thanks are particularly due to STEWART KYD, JOHN BAILEY, and JOSEPH CHITTY, Efqrs. for the information we have drawn from their ingenious labours.

The Law of
BILLS OF EXCHANGE,
PROMISSORY NOTES,
BANK-NOTES, BANKER's NOTES,
DRAFTS, AND CHECKS.

CHAP. I.

Of the Origin, Antiquity, and various Kinds of Exchanges.

AT a very early period, nature pointed out the simple Origin of exchanging one commodity for another. mode of bartering or exchanging one commodity for another, by a vague and inaccurate estimation of their respective values. The inconvenience and uncertainty of this kind of traffic occasioned the introduction of a common standard, under the denomination of money, to which every thing else should be referred as its measure or criterion.

The progress of mankind, from barter of commodities Progress from barter to money. to the invention of money, in the common transactions of life, must have been very rapid, for we find Abraham giving "400 shekels of silver *current money with the merchant*," for the field of Machpelah. *Gen. c. xxiii. v.* 16.

The exchange of money is of great antiquity, as appears Exchange of money. from the Hebrew customs, as well as from those of the Romans.

On the first day of the month Adar, which answers to our February, proclamation was made throughout all Israel, that the people should provide their half shekels, (an antient Jewish coin equal to about 2*s.* 6*d.* sterling.) which were yearly paid towards the service of the temple, according to the commandment of God. On the 25th of Adar they brought tables into the outer court of the

temple

temple where the people stood. *Exod.* xxx. 31. On these lay the lesser coins, which were to furnish those who wanted half shekels for their offerings, or who wanted smaller pieces of money in their payment for oxen, sheep, doves, &c. which stood there ready in the same court to be sold for sacrifices. But this mode of supply, and furnishing the people from these tables, was not without an exchange for other money, or other things in lieu of money, and that at an advantage. Hence also those who sat at the tables were called bankers, or masters of the exchange. *Molloy, lib.* 2. *c.* 10. *f.* 1.

How long in use among the Romans

By the Romans the exchange of money is supposed to have been in use upwards of two thousand years; money being then fabricated out of gold and silver, to avoid the carriage of merchandizes in barter from one country to another. So other nations, imitating the Jews, and Romans, erected mints and coined monies. *Molloy, lib.* 2. *c.* 10. *f.* 2.

Bills of exchange introduced by the Jews.

But it was reserved for an oppressed people, considered as the outcasts of mankind, urged by the necessity of their situation, to introduce a method by which the merchants, of regions the most remote from each other, could convey the means of procuring the value of their commodities, without the inconvenience of transporting gold or silver. About the middle, or towards the end of the thirteenth century, the Jews, driven by the exactions of the prince, from England and France, took refuge in Lombardy, and from thence gave to merchant strangers and travellers, secret letters on those to whom they had entrusted their effects in the former countries; who honourably discharged the trust reposed in them, by complying with the orders contained in the letters.—In the course of time these letters received a form, and had conferred on them the name of *Bills of Exchange. Montesquieu, lib.* 21. *c.* 16. *Kyd's Treatise, c.* 2. *p.* 2.

Further observations on the introduction of bills of exchange.

Some authors have attributed the invention to the Florentines, when, being driven out of their country by the faction of the Gebelins, they established themselves at Lyons and other towns. On the whole, however, there is no certainty on the subject, though it seems clear that foreign bills were in use in the fourteenth century, as appears from a Venetian law of that period; and an inference drawn from the statute 5 *Rich. II. f.* 1, 2. warrants the conclusion that foreign bills were introduced into this country

country previous to the year 1381. *Claxton v. Swift.*
2 Show. 485.

The mode of tranfmitting money from one country to *When uni-*
another, by means of thefe inftruments, being once dif- *verfally*
covered, the advantages derived from it foon induced *adopted.*
merchants univerfally to adopt it; and from thence it
early grew into cuftom, which feems to have been judi-
cioufly fanctioned in this country at a very early period of
our hiftory, though no earlier decifion relative to the cuftom can be found than that in 10 *Jac. I.* where it was adjudged, that an *acceptance* raifed an *affumpfit* in law, for
the breach of which an action on the cafe would lay. *Cafte*
v. Taylor. Cro. Jac. 306. 1 *Rol Abr.* 6.

It was once fuppofed that no perfon, who was not a *Perfons in*
merchant, or engaged in fome trade, could be party to a *general*
bill; but it has been long fettled that all perfons, having *competent.*
capacity and underftanding to contract in general, may
be concerned in the negotiation of thefe inftruments. *Carth.*
282. *Salk.* 125.

The perfon who writes the bill is called in law the *Of the par-*
drawer; and he to whom it is addreffed the *drawee*; the *ties.*
third perfon, or negotiator, to whom it is payable, whether
fpecially named, or the *bearer* generally, is called the *payee.*
When a bill or note is indorfed, the perfon indorfing it is
called the *indorfer*; the perfon to whom it is indorfed the
indorfee. *Black. Com.* 11, 466.

A bill or note cannot be made payable to any perfon *To whom a*
who is incapable of fuing for its payment. It cannot pro- *bill can be*
perly be made or indorfed by, nor can a bill be properly ad- *made pay-*
dreffed to any perfon incapable of making himfelf refponfi- *able.*
ble for the payment.

CHAP. II.

Of Bills of Exchange, and Promiffory Notes.

A BILL of Exchange, fays Savary, is a piece of paper *Of bills of*
commonly long and narrow, on which is written a fhort *exchange.*
order, given by a banker, merchant, trader, or other
perfon, for paying to fuch a perfon, or to his order, and
alfo, in fome countries, to the bearer in a diftant place,
a fum

a sum of money equivalent to that which such banker, merchant, or trader has received in his dwelling place. *Savary's Dict. tit. Lettre de Change.*

Form not essential.

The form, however, is not an essential part of it, for the same strictness and nicety are not required in penning bills current between merchant and merchant, as in deeds, wills, &c. *New Abr. 606.*

Nor particular words.

No particular words are necessary to make a *bill or note*; any order or promise, which from the time of making it cannot be complied with or performed without the payment of money, is a bill or a note. In the case of *Morris* v. *Lea*, plaintiff sued as indorsee upon a note by which the defendant promised to be accountable to *A*, or responsible for it to him or order, is a *good bill or note. Lord Raym.* 1396. *Str.* 629. 8 *Mod.* 362.

Must be in writing.

It is requisite that bills of exchange and notes should be in writing, and drawn by the party, or those having legal authority from him; and such drawing raises a contract to pay the same, without reference to any other transaction, promise, or obligation between the parties, whereby a pretence may be made for dishonouring the bill when due. 3 *New Abr.* 606. *Garth* 510.

Contracts of infants void, and of married women voidable.

With respect to the competency of the contracting parties, the law has in general rendered the contracts of infants *voidable*, and those of married women absolutely void. These privileges and protections are given as shields and not as swords, and therefore infants may contract for necessaries; for they would otherwise be in worse circumstances than persons of full age. *Burr.* 1801. 2 *Atk.* 35.

Of infants.

It may however be doubtful whether a bill of exchange, given by an infant for necessaries, would have the usual operation of that instrument against him; for although it has been decided that a single bond, or bond without a penalty, will bind an infant, when given for necessaries; yet if a bill of exchange, considered as a contract, were to have an obligatory force on an infant, it might, from its assignable quality, when in the hands of a third person, preclude the infant from disputing the value of the necessaries, and operate like the statement of an account, which it has been adjudged will not bind him. *Ash. En.* 273. 1 *Rol. Abr.* 729. *p* 8. *Caf. in L. and E.* 185.

A promise made after age.

An infant may, however, by a promise to pay the bill, made after he attains twenty-one, render it as operative against him as if he had been of age at the time it was made. *Sol. Ca.* 166, 201.

Although

Although it has often been decided that married women may contract so as to bind themselves, provided they live apart from their husbands, and have a permanent maintenance secured to them by deed; yet the authority of these decisions have been questioned of late, by high legal authority. 4 *Durnf. & East*, 361, 766. 5 *Durnf. & East*, 679. 6 *Durnf. & East*, 604. *Esp. C. N. P.* 6. But although the drawer, indorser, or acceptor of a bill is incapable of binding himself, such bill will nevertheless be valid against all other competent persons. *Poth. p.* 29. 2 *Atk.* 181, 2. *Chitty*, 20, 21. _{Of a married woman, living apart from her husband.}

A bill of exchange may be defined to be an open letter of request, and a promissory note a written promise, for the payment of money *absolutely*, and at all events; the one owing its existence and privileges to the law and custom of merchants; the other to the 3d. and 4th. *Anne c.* 9. which enacts, that, after May 1, 1705, all notes in writing shall have the same effect as inland bills of exchange. _{Bills and notes in some respects the same.}

A bill or note must purport the money mentioned in it shall be payable absolutely; if it purports to make the payment depend on any uncertainty or contingency, the instrument is not a bill or note. _{Not to depend upon a contingency.}

Thus an order or promise of payment out of the money, *when received*, or the produce of merchandize, *when disposed of*, is no bill of exchange; because of the *uncertainty* whether one will be *received*, or the other *disposed of*; or that its produce, when disposed of, would be sufficient. *Black.* 782. 3 *Wils.* 207. _{Or be conditional.}

A promissory note to pay money within so many days after the defendant should marry, was, on consideration, held not to be a negotiable note within the statute. 2 *Str.* 115.

So where a bill drawn by an officer on his agent, requiring him to pay so much out of his growing subsistence, was held to be no bill of exchange, nor the drawer liable, though he accepted such bill; for it concerns neither trade or credit, but is to be paid out of the growing subsistence of the drawer: so that if the party die, or the fund be taken away, the payment is to cease and determine. *Lord Raymond*, 1361. _{Drawn by an officer.}

Kingston v. *Long*, *M.* 25 G. III. The plaintiff brought an action as indorsee against the defendant as acceptor, upon an order importing to be payable, *provided the terms mentioned in certain letters written by the drawer were*
complied

complied with, and the court held clearly that the plaintiff could not recover, though the acceptance admitted a compliance with the terms, for the order was no bill, untill after such compliance; and if it were not a bill when drawn, it could not afterwards become one.

Out of rents An order to pay a sum out of rents or other money in the hands of the person to whom it is addressed, is no bill, because it may be that he has not rent or other money in his hands sufficient to discharge it. *Str.* 591.

To pay when a person is of age. An order or promise to pay when *A. B.* shall come of age, specifying the day when that event is to happen, is a good bill or note, because it is payable though he die in the interim. As in the case of *Gofs* v. *Nelson.* Action on a note payable to an infant, " when he (the infant) should come of age, to wit, 12 June, 1750;" and it was objected in arrest of judgment that it was uncertain whether the money would ever have been payable, because the infant might have died under 21; but the court held it a good note, because it was payable at all events on the 12th June, 1750, though the infant should have died before that time. *Burr.* 226.

Half-pay in advance. An order to pay money as *the drawer's quarter's half-pay by advance* before the pay will be due, is a good bill, because it will be payable though the half-pay shall never become due. *Str.* 762. *L. Raym.* 1481.

Another contingency An action was brought on the following note " I promise to pay to *T. M.* 50*l.* if my brother doth not pay it within six weeks," and after verdict for the plaintiff the court reversed the judgment, because the maker was only to pay it on a contingency. *Appleby* v. *Biddulph,* 8 *Mod.* 363. 4 *Vin.* 240. *p.* 16.

Bills, &c. must be for money only. Bills and notes must be for the payment of money *only*; an order or promise to pay money, and to *do some other act,* is not a bill or note.—On error from the court of Common Pleas, the court of King's Bench held, that a note to deliver up horses and a wharf, and pay money at a particular day, was not a note within the statute, and reversed the judgment which had considered it as such. *Martin* v. *Chauntry, Str.* 1271.

And bills and notes must also be for the payment of money in specie: an order or promise to pay in *good East India bonds* is not a bill or note. A written promise to pay 300*l.* to *B.* or order in three good *East India* bonds, was held not to be a note within the statute. *Bull. Ni. Pri.* 272. *Anon.*

A note

A note was given in these words, "borrowed of *I. S.* 50*l.* which I promise *not* to pay:" and per Lord Macclesfield, the word *not* shall be rejected, for a man shall never say, I am a cheat and have defrauded. Cited by Lord Mans. in *Ruffel* v. *Langstaffe. M.* 21 *G. III.* *A promise not to pay.*

A note so far resembles a bill that it is for the payment of money absolutely, and at all events, and when transferred it is exactly similar to a bill of exchange. But in the case of *Heylin* v. *Adamson*, it was held by Lord Mansfield, that while a note continues in its original shape of a promise from one man to another, it bears no similitude to a bill; but when it is indorsed, the resemblance begins; for then it is an order by the indorser upon the maker to pay the indorsee, which is the very definition of a bill: the indorser of the note corresponds to the drawer of the bill; the maker to the drawee or acceptor; and the indorsee to the payee, or party to whom the bill is made payable. All the authorities, and particularly Lord Hardwicke in the case of *Hamerton* v. *Mackarell, M.* 10 *G. II.* put promissory notes on the same footing with bills of exchange. *Burr.* 669. *Notes becoming similar to bills.*

And in *Brown* v. *Harraden*, where the court decided that three days grace should be allowed on promissory notes, Lord Kenyon observed, that the effect of the statute was that notes were wholly to assume the shape of bills; and *Buller* J. added, that the language of the preamble to the act was expressly that it was the object of the legislature to put notes exactly on the same footing with bills. See 4 *Durnf. & East*, 148, and 5 *Durnf. & East*, 482. *And considered in the same light.*

It has been a point much agitated whether it was necessary that a bill or note should import to have been given for *value received*; but that question was settled in the negative in the case of *White* v. *Ladwick, K. B. H.* 25 *G. III.* A declaration on a bill of exchange was demurred to, because it was not stated to have been given for value received; but the court said it was a settled point, that it was not necessary, and gave judgment for the plaintiff. See also *L. Raym.* 1471. *The words value received not neceffary,*

To entitle, however, the holder to recover interest and damages against the drawer and indorsee, in default of acceptance or payment, a bill must contain the words value received: the inserting of these words is therefore in all cases advisable. 9 & 10 *W. c.* 17. 3 & 4 *Anne c.* 9. *Except to recover interest against the drawer,*

3

A bill

A bill payable at fight differ- ent from one on de- mand.

A bill payable at fight is not to be confidered as a bill payable on demand. *Anfon* v. *Thomas*, T. 24 G. III. In an action on an inland bill, the queftion was, whether it was included under an exception in the ftamp act of 23 G. III. c. 49. f. 4. in favour of bills payable on *demand*; and the court held it was not; and Buller J. mentioned a cafe before Willes, C. J. in London, in which a jury of merchants was of opinion, that the ufual days of grace were to be allowed on bills payable at fight. A note or bill *on demand* is payable immediately.

Altering a bill

If while a bill is in the hands of the payee, or other holder, or in any cafe, it is *altered* in any material refpect, as for inftance, in the date or fum, without the confent of the drawer, it will difcharge him, although the bill may afterwards come into the hand of an indorfee not aware of the alteration. And if it is altered after acceptance or indorfement, without the acceptor's or indorfer's affent, fuch alteration fhall have the fame operation. 4 *Durnf. & Eaft*, 320. 5 *Durnf. & Eaft*, 367.

Before ac- ceptance or indorfe- ment.

But if it is altered before acceptance or indorfement, the acceptor or indorfer cannot take any advantage of the alteration; and the confent of any one of the parties to the alteration, will in general ftop him from taking advantage of it. In fuch cafe, however, a new ftamp will be neceffary, if the alteration was made after the bill was negotiated, or after it was due. *Bailey's Sum.* 24.

An altered note or bill requires a new ftamp.

A bill or note altered (though by the confent of all parties) after it has once iffued, or after the time when it was originally payable, requires a new ftamp. In the fittings after Michaelmas term, 1796, before Lord Kenyon, *Wilfon* v. *Juftice*, a bill payable originally nine months after date, was, by confent of all parties, a fortnight after it had been in the hands of the payee, made payable 12 months after date; and Lord Kenyon held that the alteration made a new ftamp neceffary, and nonfuited the plaintiff. *Bailey*, 24.

Of drawing, accepting, or indorfing by procura- tion.

Wherever a man has legally a power, as owner, to do a thing, he may confequently, as incident to his right, do it by attorney or agent. Hence it is clear that a perfon may draw, accept, and indorfe a bill by his agent as well as by himfelf. In thefe cafes, he is faid to draw, accept, or indorfe by *procuration*. As the doing of either of thefe acts is the execution of a mere minifterial office, infants, feme coverts, perfons attainted, outlawed, ex-
com-

communicated, aliens, and others incapable of contracting in their own right, so as to bind themselves, may be agents for these purposes. *9 Co. 75. b. Molloy, b 2. c. 10. 6 Mod. 96. 12 Mod. 346, 564. 3 & 4 Anne, c. 9. f. 1. Beawes, pl. 89. Co. Lit. 52. a.*

If a person signs his name upon a blank paper, stamped with a bill stamp, and delivers it to another person to draw such bill as he may choose thereon, he is the drawer of any bill to which the stamp is applicable which such person may draw thereon. *Collis v. Emet. 1 H. Black. 3. 3.* Emet signed his name upon a blank paper stamped with a shilling bill stamp (the highest stamp then used for bills) and delivered it to Livesay and Co. that they might draw thereon such bill as they should please. They drew one for 1551l. at three months date, which was duly transferred to Collis and Co. and Collis and Co. sued Emet thereon. A special verdict was found, principally with a view to another point, and the Court held Emet answerable, and the plaintiff had judgment. *Bailey's Sum. 14.*

[side: Signing a name on a blank paper]

A bill of exchange is to be considered as a simple contract debt, in a course of administration, which an executor or an administrator cannot discharge before debts by bond, without being guilty of a *devastavit*. *3 New. Abr. 601.*

[side: Not to be paid by executors, &c. before bonds.]

CHAP. III.

Of Foreign Bills of Exchange.

BILLS of Exchange are either *foreign* or *inland*; *foreign* when drawn by a merchant, residing abroad, upon his correspondent in England, or *vice versa*; and *inland* when both the drawer and the drawee reside within the kingdom. Formerly foreign bills of exchange were much more regarded in the eye of the law than inland bills, as being thought of more public concern in the advancement of trade and commerce: but now inland bills of exchange are put upon the same footing as foreign ones; what was the law and custom of merchants with regard to the one, and taken notice of merely as such, being by

[side: Of foreign bills of exchange.]

C   the

the ftatutes exprefsly enacted with regard to the other ; fo that there is now in law no manner of difference between them. *Blag.* 4. *Chitty's Tr.* 15.

Inland bills. By various judicial decifions, and by two ftatutes enacted on the fubject, the 9 & 10 *W. III, c.* 17. and the 3 & 4 *Anne, c.* 9. this doctrine feems now eftablifhed.

A fet of bills. In the cafe of foreign bills, it is ufual to make three of the fame tenor and date, in order that the bearer, having loft one, may receive his money on the other. But if the drawer only gives one, he will, if it fhould be loft, be obliged to give another of the fame tenor to the lofer. Thefe bills of the fame tener and date, are called a fet ; and each part contains a condition that it fhall be paid provided the others are not. *Poth. pl.* 39.

Condition to be inferted in each. The condition fhould be inferted in each part, and fhould in each mention every other part of the fet; for if a man, intending to make a fet of three parts, fhould omit the condition in the firft, and make the fecond with a condition mentioning the firft only, and in the third alone take notice of the other two (as pointed out by Molloy, Malynes, and Marius,) he might perhaps in fome cafes be obliged to pay each; for it would be no defence to an action on the fecond, that he had paid the third, nor to an action on the firft that he had paid either of the others. *Bailey's Tr.* 15. *Chitty's Sum.* 46.

To whom delivered. When a bill thus confifts of a fet, or feveral parts, each muft be delivered to the perfon in whofe favour it is made, (unlefs one is forwarded to the drawee for acceptance, and in that cafe the reft muft be fo delivered) otherwife there may be difficulties in negotiating the bill, or enforcing payment. *New. Abr.* 603. *Molloy, b.* 2. *c.* 10. *f.* 10. *Bailey's Sum.* 15.

Name to be properly fpelled. Care muft be taken that the name be properly fpelled ; and where there are two perfons of the fame name, the payee fhould be defcribed in fuch a manner as to prevent any miftake. 4 *Durnf. & Eaft,* 28.

Ufance. Though foreign bills are frequently drawn payable at ufance or ufances, yet they, like inland bills, may be drawn payable at fight, at days, weeks, months, or years, after fight or date, or on demand : bills, however, are feldom drawn payable on demand; but ufually, where it is intended they fhould be paid immediately, are drawn payable at fight. When drawn at fight, the drawer of a foreign bill fhould mention it to be payable according to the courfe of exchange at the time of making it, or the

drawee

drawee muſt pay according to the exchange of the day when he has ſight of the bill. "*En eſpeces au cour de ce jour.*" *Poth. pl.* 174.

Inſtead of an expreſs limitation by months or days, we continually find the time on bills drawn or payable at cer-tain places limited by the *uſance*, that is, the uſage be-tween thoſe places and this country. Uſance is the time of one, two, or three months after the date of the bill, ac-cording to the cuſtom of the places between which the ex-changes run. *[Uſance dif-ferent in different countries.]*

As *uſances* vary according to the cuſtoms of different countries, it is always neceſſary that the uſance of the place ſhould be particularly deſcribed; for where the plain-tiff declared on a bill of exchange drawn at *Amſterdam,* payable at *London,* at *two uſances,* and did not ſhew what the two uſances were; judgment was given for the defend-ant, becauſe the court could not take notice of foreign uſances which vary, being longer in one place then in another, unleſs the uſance of that particular country had been ſhewn and proved. 1 *Salk.* 132. *[The uſance ſhould be particularly deſcribed.]*

Uſance between London and any part of France, is thirty days after date.—Between London and the follow-ing places, one calendar month after the date of the bill, *viz.* Hamburgh, Amſterdam, Rotterdam, Middleburgh, Antwerp, Brabant, Zealand, and Flanders—Between Lon-don and Spain and Portugal two calendar months—Be-tween London and Genoa, Leghorn, Milan, Venice, and Rome, three calendar months.—The uſance of Amſter-dam, on Italy, Spain, and Portugal, is two months.—On France, Flanders, Brabant, and on any place in Holland or Zealand, is one month—On Frankfort, Nuremberg, Vienna, and other places in Germany, on Hamburg and Breſlau, fourteen days after ſight, two uſance twenty-eight days, and half uſance ſeven. *Kyd's. Tr.* 4. *[Different uſances par-ticularized.]*

A double uſance is double the accuſtomed time; an half uſance, half the time. *[Double uſance.]*

Where it is neceſſary to divide a month, an half uſance ſhall contain fifteen days, notwithſtanding the in-equality in the length of the months. *[Half uſance.]*

Where the time, after the expiration of which a bill is made payable, is limited by months, it muſt be com-puted by calendar, not lunar months: thus, on a bill dated the firſt of January, and payable at one month after date, the month expires on the firſt of February. *Kyd's Tr.* 5 *[Calendar months.]*

C 2   By

Of calculating

By the cuftom of merchants, where a bill is payable at fo-many days after fight, or from the date, the day of prefentment or of the date is excluded.

Old and new ftyle.

There are eleven days difference between the old and new ftyle; or, in other words, the firft day of any month, according to the *old* ftyle, is the twelfth according to the *new*. The *old ftyle* prevails in Mufcovy, Denmark, Holftein, Hamburgh, Utrecht, Gueldres, Eaft Friefland, Geneva, the Proteftant Principalities of Germany, and the Proteftant cantons of Switzerland. The *new ftyle* is followed in all the dominions of *George III.* in Amfterdam, Rotterdam, Leyden, Haerlem, Ghent, Bruffels, Middleburgh, Brabant, and all the Netherlands, except Utrecht and Gueldres. It is alfo obferved, in France, Spain, Portugal, Italy, Hungary, Poland, the Popifh Principalities of Germany, and the Popifh Cantons of Switzerland.

After date.

When a bill, payable after date, is drawn at a place ufing one ftyle, and remitted to a place ufing the other, the time is computed according to that of the place where drawn.

Sight.

A bill payable after fight muft evidently be computed according to the ftyle of the place where it is payable.

Days of grace allowed in different countries.

By the cuftom of merchants, a perfon to whom a bill is addreffed, is allowed a fhort time for payment, beyond the term mentioned in the bill, called *days of grace*. But the cuftom of thefe varies, according to the cuftom of different places. The united kingdoms of Great Britain and Ireland, Vienna, and Bergamo, *three days.* Frankfort, out of the time of the fair, *four days.* Venice, Amfterdam, Rotterdam, Middleburgh, Antwerp, Cologn, Breflau, Nuremberg, and Portugal, *fix days.* Leiplia, Naumburg, and Augfburgh, *five days.* Dantzick, Koningfberg, and France, *ten days.* Hamburgh and Stockholm, *twelve days.* Naples *eight,* Spain *fourteen,* Rome *fifteen,* and Genoa *thirty days.* Leghorn, Milan, and fome other places in Italy, no fixed number. *Kyd's Tr. 9.*

Sunday.

At Hamburgh, but no where elfe, the day on which the bill falls due, makes one of the days of grace. In England, if the third day of grace fhould happen to be Sunday, the bill is to be paid on Saturday.

Of ftamping foreign bills.

Though none of our acts of parliament require any ftamp on a foreign bill made out of this country, yet as the courts will take notice of the revenue laws of a foreign country, and will refort to the laws of the country in

4   which

which the inftrument was made, every bill muft be ftamped as required by the laws of the country where made, or otherwife the holder cannot recover upon it. *Alves* v. *Hodgfon.* 7 *Durnf. & Eaft, Efp. Ca. Ni. Pri.* 5a8.

If a holder of a foreign or inland bill of exchange, or check, transferable by *mere delivery*, lofes or is *robbed* of it, and it gets into the hands of a perfon who was not aware of the lofs or robbery, for a good confideration, previoufly to its being due; fuch perfon, notwithftanding he derived his intereft in the inftrument from the perfon who found or ftole it, may maintain an action againft the acceptor, or other parties to the inftrument; and the original holder who loft it will forfeit all right of action. *Good.* v. *Col.* 4 *Durnf. & Eaft,* 8a5. *Doug.* 633. *Chitty's Tr.* 1a4.

Lofing or being robbed of a bill.

CHAP. IV.

OF ACCEPTANCE.

THE term acceptance applies only to bills, for a note may be confidered on comparifon with a bill, as accepted when it iffues. a *Black. Com.* 470. Therefore nothing under this head is applicable to promiffory notes.

Acceptance what.

An acceptance is an engagement to pay a bill accord-ing to the tenor of the acceptance, and a general accept-ance is an engagement to pay according to the tenor of the bill. And by the cuftom of merchants, an accept-ance as effectually binds the acceptor, as if he had been the original drawer; and, having once accepted it, he cannot afterwards revoke it. *Cro. Jac.* 308. *Bailey's Sum.* 4a.

Is an engagement to pay.

Acceptance may either be written or verbal; if the former, it may either be on the bill itfelf, or in fome collateral writing. In an action againft the acceptor of a foreign bill of exchange, it appeared that the accept-ance was by a letter, in which the defendant faid, I will pay it, if you firft let me fend to my correfpondent in Ireland. This was held as well as if the acceptance had been on the bill itfelf. *Wilkinfon* v. *Lutwidge,* 1 *Str.* 648.

May be written or verbal.

It

Written or parol acceptance. It may be *verbally*, or in *writing*. On account of the ambiguity of the ſtatutes, 9 & 10 *W. III. c.* 17, and 3 & 4 *Anne c.* 9. it has formerly been ruled that an acceptance by parol was not ſufficient. But that point is now finally ſettled by a ſolemn determination in the King's Bench in the time of Lord Hardwicke. In an action againſt the defendant as acceptor of a bill, the acceptance appeared to be by parol only; which Lord Hardwicke, C. J. ruled to be ſufficient; but *Eyre,* C. J. of the Common Pleas having ruled it otherwiſe, in *Reo.* v. *Meggott, H.* 7 *G. II.* an application was made for a new trial, and the court to ſettle the point ordered it to be argued: upon the argument the court held Lord Hardwicke's directions right, and Eyre, C. J. waived his opinion and agreed with the court of King's Bench. And this determination is referred to and approved in *Julian* v. *Shobrooke,* 2 *Wilſ.* 9. and *Powell* v. *Monnier.* 1 *Atk.* 612.

Lord Mansfield ſays a verbal acceptance is binding; and in *Sproat* v. *Matthews,* it was taken for granted by the court and bar, that a parol acceptance was good. 1 *Durn. & Eaſt,* 182. See alſo *Str.* 817.

What amounts to an acceptance. A very ſmall matter will amount to an acceptance, and any words, except thoſe which put a negative on the requeſt will be ſufficient: as *accepted,* or *accepted by me A. B.* or *acc.* or *I accept the bill.* Or if the party underwrites the bill, *preſented* ſuch a day, or only the day of the month, this is ſuch an acknowledgement of the bill as amounts to an acceptance. 3 *New. Abr.* 610. *Comb.* 401.

A direction to a third perſon to pay a bill is a complete acceptance.

Date to acceptance. Where it is an acceptance of a bill payable after ſight, it is uſual to write the day on which the acceptance is made. When it is made by one partner only, on the partnerſhip account, it ſhould expreſs that he accepts for ſelf and partner; and when by an agent for his principal, it is uſual and neceſſary for him to ſpecify that he does it as agent, as otherwiſe it will make him perſonally reſponſible. 1 *Str.* 955.

What amounts to an acceptance. If the party ſays, "leave your bill with me, and I will accept it," or, "call for it to-morrow and it ſhall be accepted:" theſe words, according to the cuſtom of merchants, as effectually bind, as if he had actually ſigned or ſubſcribed his name according to the uſual manner.

                                         But

But if a perfon fays, " leave your bill with me, and I What does not, will look over my accounts and books between the drawer and me, and call to-morrow, and accordingly the bill fhall be accepted:" This does not amount to a complete ac-ceptance; for the mention of his books and accounts fhews plainly that he intended only to accept the bill, in cafe he had effects of the drawers in his hands; and fo it was ruled by Lord Chief Juftice Hale. *Molloy, b. 2. c. 10. f. 20.*

A modern reporter of fome authority informs us that, A written refufal to accept. an exprefs refufal to accept, written on a bill, is an ac-ceptance. In *Anne* 75, is this note. *Underwriting, or indorfing the bill thus,* I will not accept this bill, is held by the cuftom of merchants a good acceptance. But by Lord Mansfield in *Peach v. Kay,* in fittings after Trinity Term 1781, it was held by the judges, that " an exprefs " refufal to accept written on the bill, where the drawee " apprized the party who took it away what he had writ- " ten was no acceptance; but if the drawee had intended " it as a furprize on the party, and to make him confider " it as an acceptance, they feemed to think it might have been otherwife." *Bailey's Sum.* 48.

An acceptance may be implied as well as expreffed: An implied acceptance. thus it may be inferred, from the drawee's keeping the bill a great length of time, or by any other act which gives credit to the bill, and induces the holder not to proteft it, or is intended as a furprize upon him, and to induce him to confider the bill as accepted. *Buller's Ni. Pri. Chitty's Tr.*

A promife to accept a bill of exchange, is the fame as A promife to accept. an actual acceptance; it will bind though the acceptor has no effects in hand, and without confideration. *1 Str.* 648.

An agreement to honour a bill of exchange is virtually an acceptance.

A *promife* to accept at a *future* period, whether made to A promife to accept. the drawer or not, as for inftance, a promife contained in a letter, to accept fuch bills as the plaintiff fhould draw on the defendant at a future day, on account of a debt due from a third perfon to the plaintiff, will in all cafes operate againft the perfon making it, as an abfolute acceptance. *Burr.* 1672. *Cowp.* 571.

A verbal promife to accept a returned bill when it fhall come back, is binding if it do come back. *Cox v. Cole-man.*

But

But an agreement to accept on certain conditions, is discharged, if the conditions are not complied with. 1 Doug.

Acceptance may differ from the tenor of the bill. An acceptance may be for a less sum than that mentioned in the bill: or it may be at an enlarged period, which is usually the case when a merchant on whom a bill is drawn has no effects of the drawer in his hands, and does not suppose he shall have any at the time of payment mentioned in the bill. 1 Str. 214. Kyd's Tr. 74.

To pay in future. A drawee may accept a bill which has no time mentioned for the payment, and which is held payable at sight, to pay at a distant period, and such acceptance will bind him. 11 Mod. 190.

Conditional acceptance. If the drawee of a bill is desirous not entirely to dishonour it, he may make such an acceptance as will subject him to the payment of the money only on a contingency, in which case the acceptance is called *conditional*, as " to pay when certain goods consigned to the acceptor, and for which the bill is drawn shall be sold;" for it would effect trade if factors were not allowed to use this caution when bills are drawn on them, before they have an opportunity of disposing of the goods. Smith v. Abbot. 2 Str. 1152.

An answer that the bill would not be accepted till a navy bill was paid, was held a conditional acceptance to pay, when the navy bill should be discharged. Pierson v. Dunlop. Cowp. 571.

The condition must be expressed If the acceptance be in writing, and the drawee intend that it should only be conditional, he must be careful to express the condition in writing as well as the acceptance; for if the acceptance should, on the face of it, appear to be absolute, he cannot take advantage of any verbal condition annexed to it. Doug. 286. Kyd's Tr. 78.

Per Lord Mansfield, if an agreement to accept is conditional, and a third person takes the bill knowing of the conditions, he takes it subject to them. Doug. 286, 289.

Partial acceptance. A *partial* acceptance, is also an acceptance varying from the tenor of the bill, as where it is made to pay part of the sum for which the bill is drawn, or to pay at a different time or place. 1 Str. 214. Comb. 453. Molloy, 283.

Illustration. Wegerstoff v. Keene. A foreign bill for £127 18s. 4d. was drawn on the defendant, and he accepted it to pay 100l. part thereof: he was sued from this acceptance, and on demurrer to the replication, insisted that a partial acceptance was

was not good within the cuftom of merchants; but the court held otherwife, and judgment was given for the plaintiff. *Str.* 214.

It may likewife vary from the tenor, in the manner in which the acceptor undertakes to pay the bill; as for in- ftance, part in money, and part in bills. In either of thefe cafes, the holder, if he means to refort to the other parties to the bill in default of payment, fhould give notice to them of fuch conditional or partial acceptance. *Mar.* 68, 85. To pay part in money.

But what is an abfolute or a conditional acceptance is a queftion of law to be determined by the court, and is not to be left to the jury. 1 *Durnf. & Eaft,* 182. A conditional acceptance becomes abfolute as foon as its con- ditions are performed.

If a bill of exchange is not accepted, an action will im- mediately lie againft the drawer, before the time when it is made payable. When not accepted.

If a bill is forged the indorfer will be liable. Two forged bills were drawn upon the plaintiff, which he ac- cepted and paid; on difcovering the forgery, he brought this action for money had and received to recover back the money, but on a cafe referved, the court held it would not lie; and Lord Mansfield faid, " It was incumbent on him to have been fatisfied before he accepted or paid them, that the bills were the drawer's hand." *Burr.* 1325. And in *Smith* v. *Cheftor,* Buller J. faid, " When a bill is prefented for acceptance, the accepter looks to the hand- writing of the drawer, which he is afterwards precluded from difputing, and it is on that account that he is liable, even though the bill is forged." 1 *Durnford & Eaft,* 655. Accepting a forged bill.

Acceptance may be made even after the time appointed for payment of the bill, fo as to bind the acceptor, though it would difcharge drawer and indorfers, unlefs due notice of non-acceptance or non-payment at the time the bill be- came due, was given; and in fuch cafe, the acceptor would be liable to pay the bill on demand. 12 *Mod.* 410. *Lord Raym.* 364, 574. *Com.* 75. Acceptance after time of payment.

If *A.* draws a bill on *B.* and *B.* will not accept it, and *C.* offers to accept for the honour of the drawer, the holder need not acquiefce, but if he does *C.* is bound. *L. Ray.* 575. 12 *Mod.* 410. And per Lord Mansfield and Yates, J. an acceptance for the honour of the drawer will bind the acceptor. *Burr.* 1672, 1674. Acceptance for the honour of the drawer.

D If

Acceptance-for the honour of the drawer.

If a perfon on whom the bill is drawn refufes to ac-cept it, any third perfon after proteft for non-acceptance may accept *fupra* proteft for the honour of the bill or of the drawer, or of any particular indorfor: if he accept for the honour of the bill or of the drawer, he is bound to all the indorfees as well as the holder: if in honour of a particular indorfor, then to all the fubfequent indorfees. *Beawes,* 456. *Kyd's Tr.* 153.

On a written acceptance by any other than the drawee, it fhould feem effential that his name fhould appear. *Bailey's Sum.* 48.

CHAP. V.

Of Protests.

Proteft what

A PROTEST is only to fubject the drawer to anfwer in cafe of non-acceptance or non-payment, nor does the fame difcharge the party-acceptor, if once accepted; for the payee, or perfon to whom payable, hath now two remedies, one againft the drawer, and the other againft the acceptor. *Molloy, b.* 2. *c.* 10. *f.* 17.

Its ufe

A proteft does not raife any debt, but only ferves to give formal notice that the bill is not accepted, or accepted and not paid; and this by the common law was and is ftill neceffary, on every foreign bill before the drawer can be charged; but it was not required on any inland-bill before the ftatute 9 & 10 *W. III, c.* 17. Nor does the want of it fince that ftatute deftroy the remedy which the party had before againft the drawer for the principal. 3 *New. Abr.* 612.

Difference between in-land and fo-reign bills.

In the manner in which notice either of non-acceptance or non-payment is given, there is a remarkable difference between inland and foreign bills: in the former, no par-ticular form of words are neceffary to entitle the holder to recover againft the drawer or indorfers the amount of the bill on failure of the drawee or acceptor; it is fuf-ficient if it appear that the holder means to give no credit to the latter, but to hold the former to their refponfibility. 1 *Durnf. & Eaft,* 170.

Ufe of pro-tefting in-land bills.

A proteft upon an inland bill is never neceffary where the bill is for the payment of lefs than twenty pounds;

and

and on fuch as are for the payment of more, a neglect to
procure it only precludes the holder from recovering,
againft the perfons entitled to notice and fpecial damages
or cofts occafioned by the non-acceptance or non-payment, and intereft. See 3 & 4 *Anne c.* 9.

But by the 9 & 10 *W. III. c.* 17. there is this exception, **Exception.**
that fuch proteft may be made on the non-acceptance of an
inland bill, if fuch bill is for the payment of five pounds
and upwards within a limited time after date, and the
value is expreffed therein to have been received, or after
an acceptance written on fuch a bill, for its non-payment.

But a proteft cannot properly be made on any other inland bills. *Lefiley* v. *Mill.* 4 *Durnf. & Eaft,* 170.

On a refufal to accept an *inland* bill, no proteft is required, any act fignifying the refufal of the drawee being
fufficient. 6 *Mod.* 80. *L. Raym.* 992.

In foreign bills certain formalities are required: if the **Formalities**
perfon to whom the bill is addreffed, on prefentment, will **required in**
not accept it, the holder is to carry it to a perfon vefted **foreign bills,**
with a public character, who is to go to the drawee and
demand acceptance in the fame manner as before, and
if he then refufe, the officer is there to make a minute on
the bill itfelf, confifting of his initials, the month, the day,
and the year, with his charges for minuting. He muft
afterwards draw up a folemn declaration, that the bill has
been prefented for acceptance, which was refufed, and
that the holder intends to recover all damages which he,
or the deliverer of the money to the drawer, or any other,
may fuftain on account of the non-acceptance: the minute
is termed the *noting* of the bill, the folemn declaration
the proteft, and the perfon whofe office it is to do thefe
acts a *Public Notary*; and to his proteftation all foreign
courts give credit. *Mal.* 264. *Mar.* 16.

The *noting* is unknown in the law as diftinguifhed from **Notice is**
the proteft; it is merely a preliminary ftep to it; and **only preli-**
though it has grown into practice within thefe few years, **minary.**
it will not in any cafe fupply the place of it. 2 *Durnf. &*
Eaft, 713. *Buller's Ni. Pri.* 271.

The demand is the material thing which muft be made **A demand**
by a notary public, to whom credit is given becaufe he **is material.**
is a public officer, and it cannot be made by his clerk,
or by any other than the notary himfelf. The proteft,
though mere matter of form, is by the cuftom of merchants indifpenfibly requifite wherever notice muft be

D 2

given;

given; and, it is said, is part of the constitution of a foreign bill, nor can it be supplied by witnesses, or oath of the party, or any other way. *4 Durnf. & East.* 175. *Lord Raymond,* 993. *Buller's Ni. Pri.* 271. *Chitty's Tr.* 91.

A copy of the bill is necessary. Where there is no notary public to make out such protest, it may be made out by any substantial inhabitant of the place, in the presence of two or more witnesses. A copy of the bill must be prefixed to all protests, with the indorsements transcribed *verbatim*, with an account of the reasons given by the party why he does not honour the bill. 37 *G. III. c.* 90.

The form of the protest must always be conformable to the custom of the country where it is made. *Poth. pl.* 155.

Stamp. Protests made in this country must, in order to their being received in evidence, be written on paper stamped with a *four* shilling stamp.

Protest to be made in regular hours. The *protest* must be made within the regular hours of business, and in sufficient time to have it sent to the holder's correspondent by the very next post after acceptance refused; for if it be not sent by that time, with a letter of advice, the holder will be construed to have discharged the drawee and the other parties entitled to notice: and *noting* alone is not sufficient, there must absolutely be a protest to render the preceding parties liable. *Buller's Ni. Pri.* 271. 2 *Durnf. & East,* 713.

But it has been recently adjudged that a copy of the protest need not be sent with the notice of non-acceptance. *Esp. ca. Ni. Pri.* 512. *Buller's Ni. Pri.* 271.

Neither is it proper that the holder should send the bill itself to his correspondent, he must retain it, in order to demand payment of the drawee when it becomes due.

Losing a bill of exchange. If a bill be left with a merchant to accept, which is lost or mislaid, he to whom it is payable is to request the merchant to give him a note for the payment, according to the time limited in the bill; otherwise there must be two protests, the one for non-acceptance, and the other for non-payment, and though such note be given, yet if the merchant happens to fail, there must be a protest for non-payment in order to charge the drawer. 3 *New. Abr.* 613.

Protest for better security. Beside the protest for non-acceptance, and non-payment, there may also be a protest for better security: this is usual when a merchant, who has accepted a bill, happens to become

come infolvent, or is publicly reported to have failed in
in his credit, or abfents himfelf from 'Change before the
bill he has accepted becomes due, or when the holder has
any reafon to fuppofe it will not be paid: in fuch cafe he
may caufe a notary to demand better fecurity, and on that
being refufed, make proteft for want of it; which proteft
muft as in other cafes, be fent away by the next poft,
that the remitter or drawer may take the proper means to
procure better fecurity. *Mar.* 27. 1 *Lord Raym.* 743.
Kyd's Tr. 139.

The proteft for non-acceptance in the cafe of an inland
bill, being, as has been already obferved, merely the means
of entitling the holder to an accumulative remedy for intereft, damages, &c. and the want of it not deftroying the
holder's right to the principal fum, as it would in the cafe
of a foreign bill, it need not be made; and, as it is faid, is
in point of practice very feldom made; but notice muft be
given of the non-acceptance, otherwife the holder takes the
rifk upon himfelf.

(margin: Ufe of a proteft on inland bills.)

The ftatutes 9 & 10 *W. III. c.* 19, and 3 & 4 *Anne c.* 9.
are in many refpects obfcure, and the comments on them
in many of the early reporters equally fo. It was foon dif-
covered from the general wording of both, that the holder
might, notwithftanding thefe ftatutes (by giving a reafonable
notice without proteft) recover againft the acceptor, the
drawer, or indorfor, the amount of the original bill; for
that the word *damages*, in thefe acts, does not mean the
original fum, that being recoverable before, but the lofs
accruing from the delay. *Kyd's Tr* 146.

(margin: Remarks on 9 & 10 W. III. c. 19, and 4 Anne c. 9.)

With refpect to what is a fufficient notice, it feems
that both in the cafe of a foreign and an inland bill, fending notice by the poft is fufficient, even though the letter
fhould mifcarry, and where there is no poft, it is fufficient
to fend by the ordinary mode of conveyance. *Saunderfon*
v. *Judge.* The holder of a note wrote to the defendant,
who was one of the indorfers, to fay it was difhonoured,
and put the letter in the poft, but there was no evidence
that it ever reached the defendant; and the court held that
fending the letter by the poft was quite fufficient. 2 *H.
Bl.* 509.

(margin: What is a fufficient notice.)

In the cafe of a foreign bill it is fufficient to fend it by
the firft regular fhip bound to the place to which it is to be
fent. 2 *H. Bl.* 565

What fhall be deemed a reafonable time, muft depend
upon the particular circumftances of each cafe, and it

(margin: Jury to determine.)

muft

must always be for the jury to say whether there has been an improper delay. *Per Eyre,* C. J. H. Bl. 569.

Respecting date and sight. In foreign bills, there is no distinction between those payable at such a time after *date,* and after *sight*; but the statute confines the benefit of protest on inland bills to those payable after *date*; so that in strictness there can be no protest on those payable after sight: and this has been lately so adjudged. *Kyd's Tr.* 149.

A protest may be made on the non-payment of coal-notes, given pursuant to 3 *G. II. c.* 26. *s.* 7.

Parties residing in the place. To such of the parties as reside in the place where the presentment was made, the notice must be given, at the farthest, by the expiration of the day following the failure; to those who reside elsewhere, by the next post. *Mar.* 2d. Ed. p. 24.

The reason of protest and notice. The reason why protest and notice are required, is merely that the parties from whom the owner received the bill, may immediately call on those who are liable to them for an indemnity; we may therefore infer, that it would be perfectly immaterial from whom the notice of non-acceptance is received, provided it be brought home to the knowledge if the party entitled to insist on the want of it. *Chitty's Tr.* 97.

Where an inland bill is protested for non-acceptance, if the protest or notice thereof is not sent within fourteen days after it is made, the drawer or indorser will not be liable to damages, &c. under the 3 & 4 *Anne,* c. 9. *s.* 5.

Protests for non-payment. If, on presentment for *payment,* the person who ought to pay the bill refuses so to do, it is in general incumbent on the holder immediately to *protest* it, if the bill was foreign; and whether foreign or inland, to give notice of the dishonour to those parties to whom he means to resort for payment, or they will be discharged from their respective obligations. The observations relative to notice of *non-acceptance* are so immediately applicable to those of *non-payment,* that it will be unnecessary to mention when such notice is requisite, or by or to whom it should be sent *Chitty's Tr.* 259.

Must be stamped. The protest for non-payment of a foreign bill, which is made by a notary public, varies in point of form, according to the country in which it is made. In England it must be stamped with a four shilling stamp: it should not bear date before the bill is due, but as it must be made on

the

the laft day of grace, it may generally bear date on that day. *Mar.* 103. 6 *Durnf. & Eaft,* 212.

In general, no perfon fhould pay in honour of another perfon, before the bill has been protefted for non-payment; and it is faid that he fhould not even then make payment before he has declared to a notary public for whofe honour he intends making it; of which declaration the notary muft give an account to the parties concerned, either in the proteft itfelf, or in a feparate inftrument. *Beawes, pl.* 53. *Mar.* 128. *Honouring another's bill.*

Protefts are abfolutely neceffary in cafe the drawee cannot be found; and notice of fuch proteft for non-acceptance and non-payment muft be given to the drawer in a reafonable time, for though the drawer is bound to the party, to whom the bill is payable, till payment be actually made, yet it is with this condition and provifo, that proteft fhall be made in due time, and a lawful and ingenuous diligence ufed for the obtaining payment of the money; and the reafon thereof is, that the drawer might have had effects, or other means of his upon whom he drew, to reimburfe himfelf the bill, which fince, for want of timely notice, he hath remitted or loft, and it were unreafonable the drawer fhould fuffer through his neglect. 3 *New. Abr.* 613. *When the drawee cannot be found.*

If a bill be drawn upon *A*, and he accepts it, and afterwards refufes payment, upon which the bill is protefted, the perfon to whom it is payable may bring feveral actions againft the acceptor and drawer; for the proteft is no difcharge of the acceptor. 3 *New. Abr.* 607. *Proteft no difcharge of the acceptor.*

With refpect to the fum which the drawer and indorfers are bound to pay, they are liable, where a bill has been protefted, not only to the payment of the principal fum, but likewife to damages, intereft, &c. 8 & 9 *W. III,* 4 *Anne c.* 9.

CHAP.

CHAP. VI.

Of Indorsements,

Or the Transfer of Bills and Notes.

Indorsement what. INDORSEMENT is a term known in law, which by the custom of merchants, transfers the property of the bill or note to the indorsee; and it is usually made on the back of a bill, and must be in writing; but the law hath not appropriated any set form of words as necessary to this ceremony; and therefore if a man write his name on the back of a bill of exchange, or *this is to be paid to I. S.* or *pay the contents to I. S.* and signs his name to it, this is a good indorsement. 3 *New. Abr.* 613. *Blag.* 11.

Signature only. The mere signature of the indorser is in general sufficient. 12 *Mod.* 192, 244. *Salk.* 126, 128, 130.

But by the 17 G. III. c. 30. *f.* 1, the indorsement of a bill or note for the payment of less than five pounds, must mention the name and place of abode of the indorsee, and bear date at or before the time of making it; and must be attested by one subscribing witness.

Indorser becomes a new drawer. The person making an indorsement, is called the indorser; the person to whom it is indorsed, is called the indorsee. If a bill or note be paid or transferred over to another person, by *delivery* only, the person paying it ceases to be a party to such bill or note; but, if he indorses it, he becomes to all intents and purposes a new drawer. *L. Raym.* 181, 930. 2 *Atk.* 182. *Burr.* 670.

Payable to order or bearer. Bills or notes payable to order, or to bearer, or containing any words to make them assignable, may be assigned so as to give the assignee a right upon the bill or note against all the antecedent parties; and bills or notes containing no words to make them assignable, may be assigned so as to give the assignee a right upon them against the assignor; but not so as to give him a right against any of the antecedent parties. *Salk.* 132.

Transfer when payable to order. To the transfer of those payable *to order*, it is necessary, in addition to delivery, that there should be something by which the payee may appear to express his order. This additional circumstance is an *indorsement*, so called from being usually written on the *back*, though an order of transfer would doubtless be equally valid if written at the bottom, or on the face of the instrument. *Kyd's Treatise,* 28.

An

An indorsement to *the order of a person,* is of the same
force as an indorsement to that person, or *his order,* and he
may maintain an action on such indorsement in his own
name; for among tradesmen this form is common, though
it be intended to be made payable to the person whose order
is mentioned. *Carth.* 403.

Indorsements are either in full or in blank: an indorsement which mentions the name of the person in whose
favour it is made, is called a full indorsement; an indorsement which does not, a *blank* one. A blank indorsement,
so long as it continues blank, makes a bill or note payable
to the bearer, but the owner may write over it what he
pleases. *Blag.* 32.

As long, however, as the first indorsement continues
blank, the bill or note as against the payee, the drawer,
and acceptor, is assignable by mere delivery, notwithstanding it may have upon it subsequent *full* indorsements.
Peake 225.

In case of a loss by theft or accident, if the bill or note
be transferrable by mere delivery, or blank indorsement,
the thief or finder may transfer it; if by a *full* indorsement
only, he cannot.

A full indorsement may restrain the negotiability of a
note.

An indorsement is restrictive, which has either express
words making it so, or is made in favour of a person who
cannot transfer. Thus an indorsement in these words,
" pay the contents to *I. S.* only; or to *I. S.* for my use
or (at least when addressed to the drawee) the within
must be credited to *I. S.*" is restrictive. *P. Wilmot,* J.
The payee may check the currency of a bill or note, by
giving a bare authority to receive the money; as " pay
to *A.* for my use." *Burr.* 1227. *Black.* 299. And per
Lord Hardwicke, in *Snee* v. *Prescott,* Bills and notes are
frequently indorsed in this manner.—" Pray pay the money
to my use," in order to prevent their being filled up with
such an indorsement as passes the interest. 1 *Atk.* 249.

Blank indorsements are more frequent than those in
full, because, if every indorsement were in full, the back
of the instrument would be soon filled up, and its nego-
ciability would be less extensive.

When not restrained by act of parliament, the transfer
may be at any time after the bill or note has issued, even
after the day of payment, or before acceptance. *Doug.*
611. 3 *Durnf. & East,* 80.

E   It

Fictitious indorsement. The validity of bills payable to a fictitious payee, have lately been frequently and fully discussed in our courts of justice; the result of which discussion seems to be, that a bill payable to a *fictitious* person *or his order*, is in effect a bill *payable to bearer*, and may be declared on as such against all the parties knowing that the payee was a fictitious person. The use, however, of these fictitious names has been highly censured, and the person indorsing the fictitious name on the bill, to give it currency, would be guilty of forgery. 3 *Durnf. & East*, 174, 182, 481. 1 *H. B.* 313. *Chitty's Tr.* 48.

Adopted by the house of Livesay and Co. and others. It has lately appeared that, in many houses, (and particularly in that of *Livesay, Hargrave,* and Co.) that in order to raise money upon bills, and to make those bills more marketable, they caused them to be drawn or dated from the country, payable to the order of a fictitious person whose pretended name they indorsed on the back; and thus giving it the appearance and effect of a bill regularly transferred in the due course of business, it went with a better face to be discounted, and was done without hesitation. One of these bills having become the subject of a most interesting litigation, has led to a decision of great importance to the mercantile world.

Illustration of the point. This case is so very generally known that a particular detail of the circumstances are unnecessary, we shall therefore give a brief relation of the substance of it. *Minel* v. *Gibson.* This case was as follows. A bill drawn by *Livesay,* and Co. on the defendant was made payable to *John White,* or order, and it was found upon a special verdict, that White was a fictitious person, that his name was indorsed upon the bill by *Livesay,* and Co. that the defendants knew when they accepted the bill that no such person as *John White,* whose indorsement was then upon the bill, existed, and that the indorsement was not made by any person of that name: the court of King's Bench thought this case decided by *Vere* and *Lewis,* and gave judgment for the plaintiffs; and on a question from the House of Lords, whether the bill might not be deemed in law payable to the bearer, *Hotham, Perryen,* and *Thompson,* barons, and *Gould,* J. gave it as their opinions that it might; but *Eyre,* C. B. and *Heath,* J. differed,— after which Lord *Kenyon,* Lord *Loughborough,* and Lord *Bathurst* spoke in favour of the judgment, and Lord *Thurlow* against it, and the judgment was affirmed without a division. 3 *Durnf. & East,* 481. 1 *H. B.* 569.

Lord

Lord *Kenyon* concluded his obfervations on this cafe to the following effect: This inftrument may fairly be confidered as a bill *payable to bearer*.

Lord Loughborough obferved that it was found by the fpecial verdict, that this bill was indorfed by the drawers. He contended that from this moment the bill was no longer payable to the order of White. Therefore his Lordfhip was of opinion that this inftrument, in its proper and its legal operation, and in the real and true ftate of the tranfaction between the parties, was a bill *payable to bearer*; that Gibfon and Johnfon, by accepting this bill, undertook to pay it to whoever fhould produce it to them with the indorfement of *Livefay*, *Hargrave*, and Co. and who had paid them a valuable confideration for it. *Blag.* 40.

The Lord Chancellor then put the queftion; whereupon the verdict of the court of King's Bench was affirmed: by which circumftance the law is now underftood to be, that if any perfon accepts a bill, knowing that the bill is payable to a perfon that is not in exiftence, fuch acceptor is bound to pay fuch bill, as a bill *payable to bearer*, which in fuch a cafe confiders all indorfees as mere cyphers. *Id.*

To the queftion propofed to the Lords on this cafe, whether the matter found by the fpecial verdict, as far as it relates to the act done by the defendants *Gibfon* and *Johnfon*, imported an *utterance of the bill, knowing it to be forged*, the lords made no decifion: perhaps from merciful motives, they did not choofe to decide on the capital part.

Before the trial of James Bolland, at the Old Bailey, in February feffions 1772, no perfon had been capitally convicted for forging, by way of indorfement, the name of a *fuppofed* perfon, or one who never had exiftence; it having been generally underftood that it was effential to the commiffion of forgery that it fhould be done *in the name of another*; and confequently that the figning of a fictitious name could not be conftrued to amount to that crime. This was the general doctrine prior to Bolland's tranfaction, and many perfons thought the law had been ftrained to extend to his offence, on account of the extreme infamy of his general character. Bolland's fate, however, has been confidered as a precedent, and proved fatal to fubfequent offenders in fictitious forgery.

To indorfe a bill with a fictitious name is forgery, though fuch indorfement was unneceffary. At the Lent Affizes

Affizes for the county of Leicefter, 1777, *Edward Tuft* was tried before Mr. Juftice *Nares* for forging an indorfement on a bill of exchange : the jury found the prifoner guilty; but the learned and humane judge, cautious of paffing fentence of death in a cafe which admitted of doubt, fubmitted to the confideration of the twelve judges, whether, upon the following ftate of facts, the commiffion was proper?

Though fuch fictitious indorfement was not neceffary. The bill of exchange was the property of one *William Weitheral*, out of whofe pocket it had been picked or loft, with other things, at *Leicefter* races. The prifoner had, the very fame night, endeavoured to negociate it at Leicefter; but being difappointed, he proceeded to *Market Harborough*, where he bought a horfe of one *John Ingram*, the landlord of the inn, and offered him this bill to change. The landlord not having fufficient cafh in the houfe, carried it to a banker's in the town, where the clerk told him that it was very good paper, for that he knew the payee who had indorfed it, and that if he (the landlord) would put his name on the back of it, it fhould be immediately difcounted. The landlord, however, not knowing the perfon from whom he had received it, refufed to indorfe it; but told the clerk that the gentleman was then at his houfe, and he would go and fetch him: accordingly he went to the prifoner, who accompanied him to the banker's. The clerk then told the prifoner, that it was the rule of their fhop never to take a difcount bill, unlefs the perfon offering fuch bill indorfed it; and therefore if he (the prifoner) would indorfe it, it fhould be difcounted. The prifoner immediately indorfed it by the name of " John Williams," which *was not his own name*, and the banker's clerk, deducting the difcount, gave him cafh for it. The prifoner, in his defence, faid he had found it. The judges were unanimoufly of opinion, that this was a forgery; for though the fictitious fignature was not neceffary to his obtaining the money, and his intent in writing a falfe name was probably only to conceal the hands through which the bill had paffed, yet it was a fraud both on the owner of the bill, and on the perfon who difcounted it. The one loft the chance of tracing his property, and the other loft the benefit of a real indorfer. *Leach's Cr. Law.*

Remarks thereon. A fictitious indorfement to a bill is clearly giving it a falfe credit, and on that principle it is given with an intent to defraud; for perfons who are accuftomed to receive bills

of

of exchange, &c. conſider every name on them as an additional ſecurity or pledge to indemnify them from loſs: but if the *real* indorſers fail, recourſe cannot be had to a *fictitious* or *imaginary* one. It therefore ſeems now almoſt a ſettled point, that to make uſe of a *fictitious* name, as a *pretended indorſer* of a bill, is *forgery with intent to defraud*.

See the caſe of *Hyam Levy*, who was convicted upon the authority of the above caſe, at the Old Bailey in October ſeſſion, 1782. See alſo the caſe of *Tatlock v. Harris.* 3 *Durn. & Eaſt*, 176.

In an indictment for forging a bill of exchange, the bill may be given in evidence, though it is not ſtamped purſuant to the ſtatutes: As in the caſe of *K. v. Hawkeſwood*. At Worceſter Lent Aſſizes, 1783, the priſoner was indicted for forging a negotiable bill of exchange, purporting to be drawn by one *Prattington* on Sir *Robert Herries*, and Co. and alſo for forging two indorſements on the ſame; the one on the firm of *Cox* and *Devy*, the other in the name of *John Hadur*. There were alſo the uſual counts for uttering it, knowing it to be forged. The fact of its being a forgery, and that the priſoner had negotiated it with a complete knowledge of the fact, were clearly proved, but the bill was not ſtamped. *Mr. Baldwin*, the priſoner's counſel, ſubmitted to the Court, that the inſtrument in queſtion, even ſuppoſing it to be genuine, was not a *legal bill of exchange*, but a piece of waſte paper, incapable of becoming the ſubject either of fraud or felony; that the party who took it, muſt at that time have known that it was not a legal bill of exchange, or he muſt have been groſsly negligent, for the defect is viſible on the face of it. Mr. Juſtice *Buller*, who tried the priſoner, held, that the ſtamp acts being revenue laws, and not purporting to alter the crime of forgery, could not effect the preſent queſtion, and the jury found the priſoner guilty: but, being a new point, he reſpited the judgment, and reſerved the caſe for the conſideration of the judges. In Eaſter Term, 1783, the judges over-ruled the objection, and determined that the conviction was right. *Leach's Cr. L* 221.

A bill or note cannot be made payable to any perſon who is incapable of ſuing for its payment.

If the perſon who has a right to transfer a bill or note die, it devolves upon his perſonal repreſentative; if he becomes a bankrupt, on his aſſignees. 3 *Wilſ.* 1.

As

All the parties liable.

As every drawer of a bill is liable to the payment thereof, so is every acceptor and indorser. Also if there are several indorsers of the same bill, the last indorsee may bring his action against the first indorser, or any of them; for the indorsement is, as it were, a new bill, or at least a warranty, as some books express it, by the indorser, that the bill shall be paid. 3 *New. Abr.* 607.

The holder may sue all parties.

The holder of the bill or note, may sue all the parties who are liable to pay the money; either at the same time, or in succession; and he may recover judgment against all, if satisfaction be not made by the payment of the money before judgment obtained against all; and proceedings will not be stayed in any one action but on payment of debt and costs in that action, and the costs in all the others in which he has not obtained judgment. *Golding* v. *Grace.* 2 *H. B.* 749.

But though he may have judgment against all, yet he can recover but one satisfaction; and if he be paid by one, he may sue out execution for the costs in the several actions against the others. 2 *Vesey,* 115.

E. 32 *G. III. Smith* v. *Woodcock,* and the same against *Dudley.* The first of these was an action by the holder against the drawer of a bill, the second against one of the indorsers. There was also another action pending by the same plaintiff against another indorsor, and a fourth against the acceptor, who had refused payment. A rule *nisi* was obtained on behalf of *Woodcock* and *Dudley,* to stay proceedings against them, upon payment of the amount of the bill and costs of these two actions. *Lewis* opposed the rule, on the ground that the costs of the other actions should also have been paid. But by the court, that is only necessary when the application for staying proceedings comes from the acceptor, who is the original defaulter, and against whom all the costs occasioned by his default may be recovered. 4 *Durnf. & East,* 691.

Purchasing a bill of exchange to extort money.

Purchasing a bill of exchange to extort money is much discountenanced by the courts. *Mr. Garrow* applied for the interposition of the court of King's Bench, in the case of an attorney who had assumed a name, and had grossly misconducted himself; he had purchased a bill of exchange, amounting to £10 17s. 6d. by discounting it, and brought a number of actions upon it against the acceptor and indorsers for the purpose of getting a bill of costs, which amounted to 46l.

3

After

After this caufe had proceeded a little way, Lord *Kenyon* defired that it might be referred to the mafter. There are, faid his lordfhip, many things done which ought not to be done, and which we cannot prevent. We do not fit here in the court of confcience or of honour, to extend the bounds of the law. We may be forry, and feel a great deal of refentment at practices which we cannot punifh. I fpeak this without prejudice to this caufe. This is not the firft inftance of the kind I have feen. When fitting at Guildhall, I recollect cafes of bills of exchange which had been taken by attornies merely for the purpofe of multiplying caufes. I felt a great deal of indignation on the occafion, but was forced to conceal it.

CHAP. VII.

OF PRESENTMENT

For Acceptance or Payment.

WHETHER the holder of a bill, payable at a certain time after the date, be bound to prefent for acceptance immediately on the receipt of it, or whether he may wait till it become due, and then prefent it for payment, is a queftion which feems never to have had a direct judicial determination: in practice, however, it frequently happens that a bill is negotiated and transferred through many hands without acceptance, and not prefented to the drawee till the time of payment, and no objection ever made on that account. *Mar.* 12, 5 *Burr.* 2671. 1 *Durnf. & Eaft,* 719. *Kyd's Tr.* 118.

But when a bill is drawn payable within a fpecified time after fight, it is neceffary, in order to afcertain the period when the bill is to be paid, to prefent it to the drawee for acceptance. 1 *H. B.* 561.

And though in other cafes it may not be incumbent on the holder to prefent it before it is due, yet it is certainly moft advifable in all cafes to get it accepted if poffible, as by that means another debtor is added to the drawer, who becomes a new fecurity, and confequently renders the bill the more negotiable. 1 *H. B.* 565. *Burr.* 2670. *Beawes, pl.* 266.

Whether the holder is bound to prefent for acceptance.

How far incumbent on the holder.

F   The

The receiver of a bill undertakes to perform certain duties.

The receipt of a bill or note implies an undertaking from the receiver, to every perfon who would be entitled to bring an action on paying it, to prefent in proper time the bill for acceptance, where neceffary, and each for payment; to allow no extra time for payment; and to give notice without delay to fuch perfon of a failure in the attempt to procure a proper acceptance or payment; and a default in any of thefe refpects will difcharge fuch perfon from all refponfibility on account of non-acceptance or non-payment, and make the bill or note operate as a fatisfaction of any debt or demand for which it was given. *Bailey's Sum. 59.*

With refpect to the time of prefenting.

With refpect to the time when bills fhould be prefented for acceptance, it was lately obferved by *Buller*, J. in the cafe of *Muilman v. D'Eguino,* that the only rule which can be applied to bills of exchange, whether the bills are foreign or inland, and whether they are payable at fight, at fo many days after fight, or in any other manner, is, that due diligence muft be ufed; and, as the drawer may fuftain a lofs by the holder's keeping it any great length of time, it is advifable in all cafes to prefent it as foon as poffible. It was further faid, that the queftion, what is a reafonable time? muft depend upon the particular circumftances of the cafe; and that it muft always be left for the jury to determine whether any laches be imputable to the plaintiff. *2 H. B.* 569., *7 Durnf. & Eaft,* 425.

Lord Mansfield's opinion.

It was faid, however, by Lord Mansfield, that what is a reafonable time for giving notice (which obfervation is doubtlefs equally applicable to the time when a bill muft be prefented for acceptance,) is partly a queftion of fact, and partly of law: it may depend in fome meafure on facts, fuch as the diftance at which the parties live, the courfe of the poft, &c. but that wherever a rule can be laid down with refpect to this reafonable time, that fhould be decided by the court and adhered to for the fake of certainty. *Tindal v. Brown.* 1 *Durnf. & Eaft,* 167.

Syderbottom v. Smith. In an action againft the indorfer of a note, *Eyre,* C. J. of the common-pleas, directed the jury to find for the defendant, becaufe the plaintiff had not proved diligence to get the money from the maker. *Str.* 649.

Allowing too much indulgence.

And in the cafe of *Gee v. Brown,* the holder of an inland bill gave the acceptor time, by intervals, from the 14th of May, when the bill became due, to the 7th of June,

June, and then sued the drawer; but there being no notice
to him, *Eyre*, C. J. held the lofs ought to fall on the plaintiff. *Str.* 792.

A prefentment either for payment or acceptance muft Muft be
be made at feafonable hours; and feafonable hours are the made at
ufual hours of bufinefs in the place where the party lives to feafonable
whom the prefentment is to be made. But a neglect to hours.
make a prefentment at a proper time, may be excufed by
illnefs, or by fome other caufe or accident.

No delay warranted by the common courfe of bufinefs is
improper, nor is any delay which is occafioned by keeping
the bill in circulation at a diftance from the place where it
is payable; but a delay by locking it up for any length of
time is improper. *Per Buller*, C. J. 2 H. B. 170.

If the drawee of a bill cannot be found at the place Where
where the bill ftates him to refide, and it appears that he drawee can-
never lived there, or has abfconded, the bill is to be con- not be
fidered as difhonoured; but if he has only removed, the found.
holder muft endeavour to find out to what place he has removed; and to make the prefentment there. *Str.* 1087.
Bailey's Sum. 58.

He fhould in all cafes make every poffible enquiry after Strict en-
the drawee, and if it be in his power prefent the bill to quiry muft
him; but if the drawee has actually left the kingdom, it be made.
will be fufficient to prefent the bill at his houfe. *Efp. Ca.*
Ni. Pri. 511.

If on prefentment, it appears that the drawee is Drawee be-
dead, the holder fhould enquire after his perfonal repre- ing dead.
fentative, and if he lives within a reafonable diftance,
fhould prefent the bill to him. *Molloy, b.* 2. *c.* 10. *f.* 34.

When a bill or check is expreffed to be payable on de- Bill or check
mand, or where no time of payment is expreffed, it is pay- on demand.
able inftantly on prefentment, which may be made immediately after it is delivered to the payee, without allowing
any days of grace; and the prefentment for payment of fuch
a bill or check muft be made within a reafonable time after
the receipt of it. *Chitty's Tr.* 146.

Upon a bill, check, or note of this kind given by way What a rea-
of payment, the courfe of bufinefs feemed formerly to al- fonable
low the party to keep it, if it was payable in the place time.
where it was given, until the morning of the next day of
bufinefs after its receipt, and to the next poft if payable
elfewhere, but not longer. Thus where a note of this kind
payable in London was given there in the morning, a pre-

F 2   fentment

sentment the next morning was held sufficiently early: a presentment at two in the afternoon too late, as will appear by the following cases.

In the case of *the East India Company v. Chitty, Str.* 1175, it appeared that at half an hour after eleven in the morning of the 18th of January, the defendant being indebted to the plaintiffs, paid to the cashier a note of *Caswell* and *Mount,* Goldsmiths in Lombard-street: they continued to pay all notes till the next day at two; and immediately after they had stopped payment, the company's servant came with the note. The question was, who should bear the loss? and upon examining the merchants it was held, that the company had made it their own by not sending it out the afternoon they received it, or at furthest the next morning; and the jury found accordingly for the defendant.

But in the case of *Appleton v. Sweetapple,* M. 23 G. III. a bill payable in London on demand, was given to the plaintiff in London at one o'clock in the afternoon, and he did not present it till the next morning. The question was, whether he presented it in time? Lord Mansfield left the point to the jury, who found for the defendant; but the court granted a new trial, because the question was a matter of law upon which the judge should have decided: the jury found again for the defendant; but against the judge's direction; a second new trial was granted, and the jury again found for the defendant; and then the court refused to interfere.

Merchants' opinion respecting the proper time of presenting checks, &c. — If it is a question of fact, it should seem that, according to the late opinions of juries of merchants, a check on a banker ought, if given in the place where it is payable, to be presented for payment the same day it is received, if the distance, or other common circumstances will allow of it: if, on the contrary, the question is to be considered as dependant on the use of merchants, as already settled by judicial decisions; the result of those decisions is, that a presentment of a draft, or banker's note, payable in the place where it was given, may be made at any time before twelve o'clock on the day after the receipt of it, or at any time within twenty-four hours after such receipt. *Esp. Ni. Pri. Bailey's Sum.* 65. *Kyd's Tr.* 45. 1 H. B. 1.

Checks, &c. should be taken for payment as soon as possible. — On the whole, the best rule in these cases seems to be, that drafts on bankers, payable on demand, ought to be carried for payment on the very day on which they are received,

ceived, if from the diftance and fituation of the parties that may conveniently be done : and when it is confidered that great part of the payments for the purchafe of ftock in the public funds, is made by the purchafers in drafts on their bankers at the inftant of making the transfer, it is certainly advifable to take the drafts for payment without delay. *Beawes,* 482. *Kyd's Tr.* 46.

Where a check or bill payable on demand is given to a *Especially if* perfon at fuch a diftance from the place where it is pay-*given at a distance.* able, that a precife rule cannot be laid down relative to the time when it muft be prefented, efpecially if peculiar circumftances attend it; the rule is generally, that it muft be prefented as foon as poffible; and the time for prefentment feems to be governed by the fame rules as regulate that within which notice of non-acceptance muft be given. 2 *H. B.* 565. *Chitty's Tr.*

In all cafes, bills for payment fhould be prefented at a *At what* reafonable time before the expiration of the day on which *hours.* they became due; and if by the known cuftom of any particular place, bills are only payable within limited hours, they fhould be prefented within thofe hours. *Bailey's Sum.* 59.

This rule is alfo faid to extend to a prefentment out of the hours of bufinefs, to a perfon of particular defcription, where, by the known cuftom of the place, all fuch perfons begin and leave off bufinefs at ftated hours. *Chitty's Tr.* 148.

In the cafe of *Wiffen v. Roberts,* a bill was dated 1ft of *Payment* November 1793, and payable three months after date; in *not demand-* an action againft the drawer it appeared that the *only* pre-*able on the fecond day* fentment for payment was on the 3d of February, which *of grace.* was only the *fecond* day of grace, and the day following was not a day of public reft; and Lord Kenyon held that the non-payment by the acceptor the day before the bill became regularly due, was not fuch a default in him as could authorife the holder to have recourfe to the drawer, and the plaintiff was nonfuited. *Efpinaffe* 261.

Upon the third or laft day of grace, and within a reafon-*On the 3d* able time before the expiration of that day, a bill or note *day of grace.* muft be prefented for payment.

If the holder makes a fecond prefentment on that day, *A fecond* the drawer or maker is entitled to infift on paying it when *prefent-* fuch prefentment is made, without paying the fees of not-*ment.* ing or protefting; notwithftanding fuch prefentment is made after the banking hours, and for the purpofe of
noting

noting and protesting. In the case of *Lesley* v. *Mills*; an
inland bill for 20l. 7s. payable 14 days after sight, became due the 24th of April 1790. A banker's clerk
Bill not to be
protested till
the day af-
ter it be-
comes due. called with it for payment in the morning, and the acceptor not being at home, left word where it lay; after
six, another of the clerks, who was a notary, noted it,
and between seven and eight the first clerk went with it
again: the acceptor tendered him the amount of the bill,
and sixpence over, but he insisted on 2s 6d. for the noting, and *that* sum not being paid, an action was brought
against the acceptor, who pleaded the tender. Lord Kenyon thought a tender of the amount of the bill, at any
time of the day it was payable, was sufficient; upon
which the jury found a verdict for the defendant. A rule
to shew cause why there should not be a new trial was
afterwards granted; and, upon cause shewn, Lord Kenyon
thought the acceptor had till the last minute of the day of
grace to pay the bill, and that it could not be noted or
protested till the following day. His lordship further observed, that, " if the acceptor was ready to pay the money
during the day that it became payable, no person could
say he would not pay. This bill becomes due the 24th of
April, and when the clerk calls in the morning the acceptor is from home. He calls in the evening, and
the money is tendered to him, but he is told he must
pay 2s. 6d. more; when the tender covered the
whole sum, in his lordship's opinion. This was a case of
which the bankers ought very seriously to consider; they
shut up at six, but other people did not shut up their shops
at six."

Buller, J. thought they were payable any time of the
last day of grace upon demand, so as such demand was
made within reasonable hours; and that they might be
protested on that day. Grose, J. declined giving any
opinion upon these points; but the whole court concurred,
that the bill in question could not be noted, because it was
payable within a limited time after sight, and the statute
authorises the noting of such inland bills only as are payable after date. The rule was discharged. 4 *Durnf. &*
East, 170.

Though a
contrary
custom still
prevails. But though this decision may have established the law,
that a bill of exchange is not to *be protested until the day*
after it becomes due, yet it has not varied or lessened the
contrary practice. Bankers contend, that the custom of
merchants having always been to protest the bill in the
evening

evening of the day it becomes due, no power less than an act of the legislature can set it aside; and since this custom produces a considerable emolument, by making one of their clerks act as a notary, the practice will not easily be given up. On the other hand, though this decision has been confirmed, and the law divested of all doubt, yet the consideration of 2s. 6d. being of small import, and the delay of payment to the last moment rather a subject of disgrace than otherwise, very few will be willing to contest the matter. *Blag. 29.*

Presentment for payment, where necessary, must be made by the holder of the instrument, or his agent, being competent to give a legal acquittal on receipt of the money, to the person in general on whom it is drawn; and a person in possession of a bill payable to his own order, is a holder for the purpose, though it was once thought he had only an authority to indorse. It is not necessary that the demand should be personal, it being sufficient if it is made at the house of the acceptor; and it is the same thing, in effect, if it be made at the place appointed by him for payment, or of his agent who has been used to pay money for him. *Esp.* 115, 512. 10 *Mod.* 286. *Poth. pl.* 129. 2 *H. B.* 509.

By whom to be presented.

Though the general rule of law is, that when computation is made *from* an act done, the day in which the act is done must be included; the law with respect to bills of exchange is different, for the custom of merchants, as judicially sanctioned, has settled that where a bill is payable at usance, so many days after sight, or date, the day of acceptance, or of the date must be excluded. 3 *Durnf. & East,* 623. *Lord Raym.* 280. *Beawes, pl.* 252.

Compensation.

If a bill drawn payable ten days after sight, is presented on the 1st of a month, the ten days expire on the 11th, and the bill, by the addition of the days of grace, becomes due on the 14th. When a bill or check is drawn payable at usance, or a certain time after date, and it is not dated, the time when it is payable must be computed from the day it issued, exclusive thereof. *Armitt* v. *Breame, Raym.* 1076. *Bailey's Sum.* 68.

The bankruptcy or known insolvency of the drawee, or maker, is no excuse for a neglect to make a presentment, or to give notice. In *Russel* v. *Langstaffe*, Lee said it had frequently been ruled by Lord Mansfield at Guildhall, that it is not an excuse for not making a demand on a note or bill, or for not giving notice of non-payment, that the

Bankruptcy of the drawee not an excuse for neglecting presentment.

drawer

drawer or acceptor was become a bankrupt, as many
means may remain of obtaining payment by the affiftance of friends, or otherwife; and Lord Mansfield, who
was in court, did not deny the affertion. 1 *Durnford &*
Eaft, 408.

Drawee dif-
honouring
bill.
If the drawee, on prefentment for acceptance, difhon-
ours the bill, the holder may infift on immediate payment
by the parties liable to him, or, in default thereof, may
inftantly commence an action againft them; on which
principle it was determined, that if a man draws a bill,
and commits an act of bankruptcy, and afterwards the
bill is returned for non-acceptance, the debt is contracted
before the act of bankruptcy, and may be proved under the
commiffion; which could not have been the cafe, if the
time when notice of non-acceptance was given had been
confidered as the period when the debt was contracted.
Doug. 54. *Buller's Ni. Pri.* 269. 2 *Str.* 949.

CHAP. VIII.

Of Promissory Notes, Bank Notes, Banker's Notes and Checks.

Promiffory
note, what.
A *PROMISSORY Note* may be defined to be a written
promife for the abfolute payment of money, drawn by the
maker upon himfelf in the nature of a bill of exchange, at
a time therein limited, or on demand, to a perfon therein
named; or fometimes to his own order, or often to the
bearer. At firft thefe notes were confidered only as written evidence of a debt; for it was held that a promiffory
note was not affignable or indorfible over, within the cuftom of merchants, to any other perfon, by him to whom
it was made payable; and that if, in fact, fuch a note had
been indorfed or affigned over, the perfon to whom it
was indorfed or affigned, could not maintain an action,
within the cuftom, againft the perfon who drew and fub-
fcribed the note; and that within the fame cuftom, even
the perfon to whom it was made payable could not maintain fuch action. *Kyd's Tr.* 18.

Promiffory
notes made
negotiable
like bills by
4 *Ann.*
But the increafe of trade, and the neceffity of paper
credit, induced bankers and others to contrive fome expedient of bringing promiffory notes within the cuftom
of

of merchants, and making them negotiable like inland bills of exchange: this question, however, agitated and exercised the judgment of the most able lawyers of the last century. But at length, in consequence of an application from the merchants, it was enacted by the 3 & 4 *Anne, c.* 9 and made perpetual by the 7th of *Anne, c.* 25. *s.* 3. " that, from the first of May 1705, all " notes in writing made and signed by any person or per- " sons, body politic or corporate, or by the servant or " agent of any corporation, banker, goldsmith, merchant " or trader, who is usually entrusted by him, her, or " them, to sign such promissory notes for him, her, or " them, whereby such person or persons, body politic " and corporate, his, her, or their servant or agent as " aforesaid, doth or shall promise to pay to any other per- " son or persons, body politic and corporate, his, her, or " their order, or unto bearer, any sum of money men- " tioned in such note, shall be taken and construed to be, " by virtue thereof, due and payable to any such person " or persons, body politic and corporate, to whom the " same is made payable; and also every such note payable " to any person or persons, body politic and corporate, " his, her, or their order, shall be assignable or indors- " able over, *in the same manner as inland bills* are or may " be, according to the custom of merchants; and that " the person or persons, body politic and corporate, to " whom such sum of money is or shall be by such note made " payable, shall and may maintain an action for the same, " *in such manner as he,* she, or they, *might do upon any* " *inland bill of exchange,* made or drawn according to " the custom of merchants, against the person or persons, " body politic and corporate, who, or whose servant or " agent as aforesaid, signed the same; and that any per- " son or persons, body politic and corporate, to whom " such note that is payable to any person or persons, body " politic and corporate, his, her, or their order, is in- " dorsed or assigned, or the money therein mentioned or- " dered to be paid by indorsement thereon, shall and may " maintain his, her, or their action for such sum of " money, either against the person or persons, body poli- " tic and corporate, who, or whose servant or agent as " aforesaid, signed such note, or against any of the per- " sons that indorsed the same, *in like manner as in cases* " *of* inland bills of exchange."

G

By

Notes are on the same footing. By this statute promissory notes are placed upon the same footing as bills of exchange, and consequently the decisions respecting the one are in general applicable to the other. Thus it has been adjudged that there is no difference between bills and promissory notes; and the latter, when payable at a stated time, are also entitled to days of grace. 4 *Durnf. & East*, 152.

In the case of *Carlos* v. *Fancourt*, the question was, whether a note payable out of a particular fund could be declared on as a promissory note, and it was decided in the negative; because promissory notes must stand or fall on the same rules by which bills of exchange are governed. 5 *Durnf & East*, 482.

But the note must be indorsed first. In *Heylin* v. *Adamson*, the question was, whether the indorsee of a bill was bound to make a demand upon the drawer as the indorsee of a note must upon the maker; and, by Lord Mansfield, while a note continues in its original shape of a promise from one man to another, it bears no similitude to a bill of exchange: but when it is indorsed the resemblance begins; for then it is an order by the indorser upon the maker to pay the indorsee, which is the very definition of a bill: the indorser becomes, as it were, the drawer; the maker of the note the acceptor, and the indorsee the person to whom it is made payable. This point of resemblance once fixed, the law relative to bills becomes applicable to promissory notes. All the authorities, and particularly Lord Hardwicke in *Hamerton* v. *Mackarell*, M. 10 G. II. put promissory notes on the same footing with bills of exchange. *Burr.* 669, 1224.

Respecting corporations Whether a corporation, which has not a special power expressly given for the purpose, can be concerned in drawing or accepting a bill of exchange, or promissory note, or in the negotiation of either, or can be made the payee, is a question which seems never to have had the consideration of a court; perhaps because nobody has ever entertained a doubt on this head; and it seems to have been taken for granted by the legislature, and it is consistent with the general principles of law, that by the intervention of an agent or servant, lawfully authorized, or corporation, on which no restraint is imposed in its original constitution, might in this respect act as a natural person. There is however a proviso in the act of 3 & 4 *Anne c.* 9, which puts promissory notes on the same footing with bills of exchange, that no body politic or corporate shall have power, by virtue of it, to issue or give out notes, by themselves or their servants, other than such as they might have

have iffued if this act had not been made. *Edie* v. Eaft India Company. *Blackft.* 395. *Burr.* 1216.

By 5 *W. & M. c.* 20. *f.* 28, THE BANK OF ENGLAND has a fpecial power, conferred on it for this purpofe.

BANK NOTES owe their introduction and eftablifhment to the following ftatutes, viz. the 5th of *William and Mary, c.* 20. *f.* 19, and 20; and the 8th and 9th of *William III, c.* 20, *f.* 30. The firft empowered the king to incorporate the perfons fubfcribing towards the raifing and paying into the receipt of the exchequer the fum of 1,200,000*l* by the name of " the Governor and Company of the Bank of England." Thefe notes are uniformly made payable on demand, and are not, as Lord Mansfield obferved, in *Miller* v. *Race,* mere fecurities, or documents for debts, nor are they efteemed as fuch; but are confidered as money or cafh in the ordinary courfe and tranfactions of bufinefs, by the common confent of mankind, which gives them the credit and currency of money to every effectual purpofe : and on payment of them, whenever a receipt is required, the receipts are always given as for money. They pafs, by will, which bequeaths all the teftator's money or cafh.

Origin of bank notes.

They are confidered as cafh.

And it was decided in Hilary term 1790, that bank notes are confidered as money, and therefore a proper tender in payment, in the cafe of *Wright* v. *Read.* Mingay obtained a rule to fhew caufe why the annuity deeds in this cafe fhould not be delivered up to be cancelled, on the ground that the true confideration was not fet forth in the memorial : part of the confideration was in money, and the reft in *bank notes* of the Bank of England; whereas the whole confideration was defcribed as money in the memorial. *Erfkine* now fhewed caufe, and faid that bank notes had always been confidered as money; they are fo in the cafe of tenders. Lord *Kenyon,* C. J. bank notes are confidered as money to many purpofes: it was fo held by Lord *Mansfield* and the court, in *Miller* v. *Race.* *Afhurft,* J. the annuity act was paffed for the purpofe of guarding againft fictitious confiderations; but it cannot be contended that the payment in this cafe is within the mifchief which that ftatute intended to remedy. Bank Notes are money to all intents, and in this inftance were taken as fuch. *Buller,* J. This court has never yet determined that a tender of bank notes is at all events a good tender: but if they have been offered, and *no objection has been made on that account,* this court has con-

And a proper tender in payment.

fidered

fidered it to be a *good tender*; and very properly fo, for bank notes pafs in the world as cafh. In a cafe on the other fide of the hall, the Lord Chancellor once fuggefted a doubt whether thefe kind of notes were money; but here we have always been inclined to confider them as fuch, though the queftion has never yet beeen diftinctly determined. 3 *Durnf. & Eaft,* 554.

Bank notes are not a legal tender, if objected to at the time of the offer; though, after fuch a tender, a creditor cannot arreft his debtor, it having been enacted, by the 38 *G. III. c.* 1. *f.* 8. that no perfon fhall be held to bail, unlefs the affidavit of the debt alledged that no offer has been made to pay the debt in bank notes payable on demand.

In bankruptcies. On bankruptcies, bank notes, cannot be followed as identical and diftinguifhable from money. If they are loft, indeed, an action of trover will lie againft the finder, by the true owner; as it will alfo for money before it has paffed in currency.

But after they have come into the hands of a third perfon, in a fair courfe of dealing, they can no more be recovered of him than money under the fame circumftances.

It has been adjudged, that an action for money had and received will not lie againft a finder of bank notes, to recover the value, unlefs money has been actually received for them. *Noyes* v. *Price* and another. *H.* 16 *G. III.*

Formal fet of words not neceffary. A formal fet of words is not effential to the validity of a promiffory note, cafh note, or Bank of England note, any more than it is to a bill of exchange. It is fufficient if it amounts to a promife to pay money. And therefore it hath been held, that a note drawn in thefe words *I promife to account with I. S. or his order for 50l. value received by me, &c.* is a good negotiable note, within the ftatute 3 & 4 *Anne c.* 9. and that the word *accopnt* fhall be conftrued the fame as to *pay*, and not to render an account as a factor or bailiff; and the rather, becaufe he is not only accountable to *I. S.* but alfo to his order; which he cannot be as a factor or bailiff, and therefore it muft be to pay the money to the indorfee, or order of *I. S. Morris* v. *Lea. Str.* 629.

But they muft convey a promife. But the mere acknowledgment of a debt, without fome words from whence a promife to pay money can be reafonably inferred, can only be confidered as evidence of a debt.

debt. Hence the common memorandum of *I O U*, has been declared not to amount to a promissory note. *Esp. Ca. Ni. Pri.* 426.

It has been adjudged that a note written by the plaintiff, **Note only signed by the party.** and subscribed by the defendant, is a note *made and signed* by the defendant within the act of 3 & 4 *Anne c.* 9. for the signing or subscribing is the lien, and the writing or making it only the mechanical part of it. *T. 6 Anne. Ash v. Baron.*

By the 23 G. III. c. 49. f. 9, and other subsequent **Bank notes exempted from stamp duty.** statutes, all promissory and other notes and bills, issued by the BANK OF ENGLAND, are exempted from any stamp-duty, in consideration of the Governors and Company paying into the receipt of his Majesty's Exchequer the annual sum of 12,000 *l.* by half-yearly payments. It is also provided, that nothing in these acts shall be construed to give legality to any bill of exchange or promissory note which was not legal before.

An order or promise to pay within a limited time after **A promise almost on a contingency.** the payment of money due from Government, is a good note, because it is morally certain that such payment will be made. *Andrew's v. Franklin.* A note payable two months after a certain ship should be paid off, was objected to, as depending upon a contingency which might never happen; but, by the court, the paying off the ship is a thing of a public nature, and this is negotiable as a promissory note: judgment for the plaintiff. *Str.* 24.

A promissory note requires no protesting, though it **A promissory note requires no protest.** may be indorsed over by a variety of people; for as there is no drawee, there can be no protest either for non-acceptance, or for non-payment. The law considers a promissory note in the light of a bill drawn by a man upon himself, and accepted at the time of drawing; and therefore, in cases of non-payment, the indorsor, or person holding the note, has his remedy against the drawer at any distance of time within six years; even though he should forget to give advice of its having been refused payment.—This is an advantage which always arises to the holder of a promissory note, which does not extend to the holder of a draft.

Bankers' Cash Notes, formerly called Goldsmiths' notes, **Banker's cash notes.** are promissory notes given by bankers, who were originally Goldsmiths. These notes were attempted to be introduced by the Goldsmiths, about thirty years before the commencement of the reign of *Anne.* They were

were countenanced by the merchants, and generally esteemed as negotiable; but Lord Holt strenuously opposed the negotiability of these, as well as of common promissory notes; and they were not generally settled to be negotiable till the stat. of 3 and 4 *Anne c.* 9, was passed, which relates to notes of the two descriptions above denominated. These bankers notes seem originally to have been given by bankers to their customers, by way of acknowledgment for having received money for their use. *Holt,* 119. 1 *Salk.* 283.

Their form and use.
These cash-notes are now seldom made or issued, except by country bankers; the introduction of checks having superseded their use. When notes are issued by London bankers, they are called shop-notes: their form is similar to that of a common promissory note, payable to bearer on demand, and are stated in pleadings as such. Being payable on demand, they are considered as cash, whether payable to order or bearer. Like bankers' checks, they are generally transferred from one person to another by delivery. Or they may be negotiated by indorfement, when the acts of indorfing will operate as the making of a bill of exchange, and the instrument may then be declared on as such, against the indorfor. In other respects they are governed by the same rules as bills of exchange. *Lord Raym.* 744. *Doug.* 635. 1 *Salk.* 132. 4 *Durnf. & East,* 149.

Notes payable to the bearer on demand.
But though the law relative to the transfer of bills of exchange is generally applicable to the transfer of promissory notes, it differs from a bill in one instance, namely, in the *time* when a transfer of it may be made: for a bill being once paid, cannot again be negotiated so as to raise any new contracts on it; but by 31 *G. III. c.* 25, notes payable to the *bearer on demand,* for any sum not exceeding 200*l.* and stamped with a proper stamp, may be *re-issued after payment* without a new stamp, if the person who made and first issued them, paid them at the place where they were first issued or negotiated. And by the same statute it is enacted, that notes of the same description, *not exceeding thirty pounds,* may be *re-issued after payment,* by whomsoever, or wheresoever they may have been paid. *Chitty's Tr.* 176.

What drafts on demand, &c. pay no duty.
By the 31 *G. III. c.* 25, No draft or order for the payment of money to the *bearer on demand,* bearing date on or before the day on which it is issued, and at the place from which it is drawn and issued, and drawn on a *banker*

acting

acting as such within *ten* miles of the place where such draft or order was actually made, is subject to any duty.

On payment of the amount of a bill or note, doubts have been entertained whether the person paying can insist upon a receipt being given; but it is usual to give a receipt on the back of the bill, which need not, like other receipts, be stamped, the legislature having perhaps supposed that the stamp upon the bill or note before it was issued, was sufficient. See 23 *G. III. c.* 9.

If a banker pay the draft of a trader keeping cash with him, after knowledge of an act of bankruptcy, the assignees may recover the money. 2 *Durnf. & East,* 113.

CHAP. IX.

OF PARTNERS AND PARTNERSHIP RESPECTING BILLS, &c.

PARTNERS are where two or more persons agree to come in share and share alike to any trade or bargain, in certain proportions agreed upon. 16 *Vin. Abr.* Tit. *Partners.* — Partners, what.

Where there are two joint traders, and a bill is drawn on both of them, the acceptance of one binds the other, if it concern the joint trade, because they trade for a common benefit; and therefore where one of them gives credit, it is the act of both. And this custom being extremely convenient to persons in trade, our courts have long given their sanction to it. 1 *Salk.* 125. *Gilb. L. E.* 117, 118. 12 *Mod.* 345. 7 *Durnf. & East,* 207. — Acceptance of one binding to both.

It has been said, however, that the act of one partner will not bind the other, if it concerns him only in a distinct interest; but it appears from other authorities that it is not material whether the bill is drawn or accepted on account of the partnership concern or not, provided the holder is not conusant of its being the act of one partner for his sole benefit; and that one partner, in the name of the firm, or of all the parties, may pledge the credit of his co-partner, or co-partners, to any amount by any act in the way of merchandize. *Peake,* 80. 2 *Vern.* 277, 292. *Esp.* 524. — How far it binds one in a distinct interest.

But

By deed. But one partner cannot bind another by deed, without an exprefs authority for fo doing. 4 *Durnf. & Eaft,* 313. 7 *Durnf. & Eaft,* 207.

Where a note or bill is drawn in favour of two or more in partnerfhip, an indorfement by one will bind both or all, if the inftrument concern their joint trade. *Kyd's Tr.* 106.

Bill drawn by two who are not partners. So, where a bill drawn by two is made payable to them or their order, it would feem from principle that either might transfer without the other; for when two perfons join in the fame bill, they hold themfelves out to the world as partners, and, for that purpofe, are to be treated as fuch; and when a bill goes out into the world, the perfons to whom it is negotiated are to collect the ftate and relation of the parties from the bill itfelf. If they appear on the bill as partners, it may be of lefs public detriment to fubject them to the inconvenience of being treated as fuch, than to permit them to deny that they are fo. *Carwick v. Vickery. Doug.* 630, 653. *Kyd's Tr.* 106.

Muft be indorfed by both. But in the above cafe, the defendant had a verdict, becaufe the inftrument was not figned by both the payees, according to the univerfal ufage and underftanding of the merchants and bankers in London.

If a factor of an incorporated company draws a bill on fuch company, and any one member accepts it, the acceptance will not bind the company, nor any other member of it, becaufe it is a private act of the party, and not a public act of the company.

On the fame principle, if ten or more merchants, each in his individual capacity, employ one factor, and he draws a bill on all of them, and one accepts it, this fhall only bind him, and not the reft, becaufe they are feparate in intereft, the one from the other. *Buller's Ni. Pri.* 279. *Beawes, pl.* 228.

On the diffolution of partnerfhip. If on a diffolution of partnerfhip between three or more partners, an authority be given to one of them to receive all debts owing to, and to pay thofe due from, a partnerfhip on fuch diffolution, this does not authorize him to indorfe a bill of exchange in the name of the partnerfhip, though drawn by him in that name, and accepted by a debtor of the partnerfhip after the diffolution. 1 *H. B.* 155.

Acceptance by one partner only. When an acceptance is made by one partner only, on the partnerfhip account, it fhould exprefs that he accepts for felf and partner, and when by an agent for his principal,

cipal, it is ufual and neceffary for him to fpecify that he does it as agent, as otherwife it would make him perfonally refponfible. *Poth. pl.* 118. *Str.* 955. 1 *Durnf. & Eaft,* 172.

On an action on the ftatute of limitations, refpecting partners, *H.* 32 *G. III. Perry* and others againft *Jackfon,* Bart. and others. This was an action on a bill of exchange for 100*l.* by the payees. againft the drawers. The declaration ftated, that the defendants on the 24th of November 1767, at New York, in parts beyond the feas, *to wit,* at *London,* &c. drew the bill in queftion, requefting *R. Willis* to pay at 40 days fight the contents to the plaintiffs: that *Willis,* in January 1768, refufed to accept, and afterwards to pay it: by reafon whereof, and according to the ufage and cuftom of merchants, the defendants became liable to pay, &c. The defendants pleaded feverally the ftatute of limitations: to which the plaintiffs replied, that when the caufe of action accrued to the plaintiffs, one of them was abroad in parts beyond the feas, and out of the kingdom of Great Britain, *to wit,* at New York in America; and that he remained fo abroad, in parts beyond the feas, continually from thence until October 1787, when he returned, &c. averring that they exhibited their bill within fix years after his return. The defendants demurred generally to thefe replications.

Baldwin and *Adam* argued in fupport of the demurrers, and Wood *entra.* Lord *Kenyon,* C. J. It is rather fingular that this is the firft time that this queftion has been brought into a court of law, though the circumftance on which the queftion arifes muft have frequently occurred. It being admitted that there is no decided cafe on this point, it muft depend on the reafonable conftruction to be put upon this act of parliament. The provifo on which the queftion arifes was introduced into this ftatute in order to protect the interefts of thofe perfons which there was no one of competent age, of competent underftanding, or competent in point of refidence in this country, to protect. Now two of the plaintiffs in this cafe have always been refident here: and it was their duty to watch over thofe interefts in which they themfelves were equally concerned with the partner who refided abroad. It is admitted that *one partner* may do feveral acts to bind the interefts of all; *he* may releafe as well as create a debt; *he* may alfo, by his acknowledgement of a debt, take a cafe out of the ftatute of limitations; and I fee no reafon why the

H   fame

same rule should not hold good in the present instance. The third section of this act of parliament limits the time of bringing actions in all cases to six years after the cause of action accrues; the plaintiffs therefore were bound to commence their action at an earlier period, unless they come within the exception of the last clause of the act, by which it is enacted, " that if any *person* or *persons* entitled to such action, &c. be beyond the seas, then such person or persons shall be at liberty to bring the same actions, so as they take the same within such time as before limited after their return from beyond the seas as other persons having no such impediment might have done." Now the words of this clause, grammatically speaking, do not apply to the present case: they only extend to cases where the person individually, a single plaintiff, or *persons* in the plural, when there are several plaintiffs, are not in a situation to protect their interests. Neither does this case come within the policy of the law which provides that, if parties neglect their interests for such a length of time as six years, they shall lose the benefit of suing to inforce their demands. I am therefore clearly of opinion, both on the words of the act of parliament, and on grounds of policy, that the plaintiffs are barred by the statute of James. *Ashurst*, J. The plaintiffs are not now entitled to recover on this bill of exchange, whether their case be considered on the words of the statute, or on the reason of the thing. The plaintiffs do not come within the words of the proviso, as my lord has already observed: and this statute having been always considered as a beneficial law for the public, we ought not to extend the exceptions in it to a case which does not require it. It was competent in the plaintiffs, *who resided in England,* to bring the action as well as to release it. And in constructing another act of parliament, *viz.* the 14 G. II. c. 17. *s.* 3. which requires ten days notice of trial where the defendant resides above 40 miles from London, we have determined, that if *one* of the defendants reside within that distance, so long a notice is not necessary. *Buller*, J. declared himself of the same opinion. *Grose*, J. absent. 4 *Durnf. & East*, 516.

Joint debts.   Lord Chancellor King was of opinion that *joint* debts could not be set against a *separate* demand due to the bankrupt; this case not being within the statute of 2 G. II. c. 22. *s.* 13.

                                            But

But generally fpeaking, as Lord Chancellor *Cowper* faid, where there was mutual credit between a bankrupt and a creditor, the balance fhould only be paid; and the claufe of the ftatute was not to be conftrued of dealings in trade only, or in cafe of mutual running accounts, but alfo where one credit was upon mortgage, and the other upon note; obferving that, in all cafes of mutual credit it was natural juftice and equity that only the balance fhould be paid. *Wilf.* 326.

Separate creditors are allowed to come in under a *joint* commiffion; but the joint effects are firft to be applied to pay the partnerfhip debts: and as to the feparate effects, firft the feparate creditors, and afterwards the partnerfhip creditors, are to be paid out of the fame. *Atk.* 67. *pl.* 22. 2 *Vern.* 706. *pl.* 628.
Separate creditors.

A gives a promiffory note for 200*l.* payable to *B*, or order; *B.* indorfes it to *C.* who indorfes it to *D.—A. B.* and *C.* became bankrupts, and *D.* received 5*s.* in the pound, on a dividend made by the affignees of *A.*—— Lord Chancellor King ordered *D.* to come in as a creditor for 150*l.* only out of *B's* effects. 2 *Wilf.* 407. *pl.* 129.

And Lord Chancellor Hardwicke was clearly of the fame opinion, upon a fimilar occafion. *Atk.* 137.

If a bill is drawn and figned by an agent, it is ufual to fign it as follows: *A. B.* for *C. D.* and if he does not mention for whom he figns, he will be perfonally liable; and if figned by one perfon for himfelf and partners, it is ufual, and perhaps neceffary, to fign it as follows: "*A. B.* for *A. B.* and Company," or to that effect.
Bill drawn by an agent.

As partners are, in a great degree, accountable for the acts of each other, it feems abfolutely neceffary that after the diffolution of their partnerfhip, they fhould give *notice* of fuch diffolution in the Gazette: by this prudent ftep the confequences are avoided of any one of the partners making, indorfing, or accepting a bill in their names. And even fuch notice is not fufficient, unlefs it be brought home to the knowledge of the holder of the bill: it will therefore be neceffary to apprize their individual correfpondents of fuch an occurrence. *Peak,* 42, 154. *Cowp.* 449.
Notice of diffolving partnerfhip in the Gazette.

CHAP. X.

OF INFANTS, FEME COVERTS, &c. RESPECTING BILLS OF EXCHANGE.

Who may draw and negotiate bills of exchange.

AS bills of exchange were first introduced for the convenience of commerce, it was formerly supposed that no person could be concerned in drawing or negotiating such an instrument who was not an actual merchant; but the multiplied concerns of society induced others, not in trade, to adopt the same mode of remittance, and it has since been decided that any person capable of binding himself by a contract may draw or accept a bill of exchange, or be in any manner engaged in the negotiation of it, and that he shall be considered as a merchant for that purpose. But it is not necessary in a declaration on a bill, to aver, that the defendant is a merchant. See *stat. 5 R. II. Lutw.* 891, 1585. 2 *Vent.* 292. 12 *Mod.* 36, 380. *Salk.* 126 *Kyd's Tr.* 28.

On the same principle, since the *stat.* 3 & 4 *Ann. c.* 9. any man, though not a merchant, may be a party to a promissory note.

Parties must be competent.

But it is essential to the validity of every contract, that there be proper parties to it, and that those parties have capacity to contract. The parties to a contract are usually only two, namely, the person binding himself to perform some act, and the person in whose favour that act is to be performed; but in the case of bills of exchange, notes, checks, &c. on account of the assignable quality, there may be, and usually are, several other parties. *Chitty's Tr.* 18.

Infants and feme coverts.

With respect to competency it may in general be observed, that the law has wisely taken care of the interests of those who either have not judgment to contract, as in the case of infants; or having contracted are incapable of performing the contract; the law in general has therefore rendered the contracts of infants voidable, and those of married women absolutely void.

From the observations made on the daily actions of infants, as to their arriving to discretion, the laws and customs of every country have fixed upon particular periods on which they are presumed capable of acting with reason and discretion: in our law the full age of man or woman is twenty-one years. 3 *Bac. Abr.* 118.

If

If a bill is beneficial to a minor, payment to him would be valid. *Poth. pl.* 166. But a payment to a married woman, after knowledge of that fact, would not discharge the person making it. *Id.* 167. Beneficial bill to a minor.

A married woman, in general, can bind herself by no contract; nor can she, without a special authority, bind her husband, except it be for such necessaries as are suitable to his rank: it is therefore clear that a bill of exchange or promissory note, to which she is a party, is of no force.

A *feme covert*, or married woman, is not to be considered as having an existence independent of her husband, though she is by particular custom, permitted to trade upon her separate account. *Black.* 1081. 4 *Durnf. & East*, 361. *Burr.* 1176. Married women may trade.

And if, in this case, she be sued in a superior court, her husband must be joined for conformity, and he may plead the custom in bar. 3 *Burr.* 1776, 1784.

A woman is considered as having an existence independent of her husband, who lives apart from him under articles of separation, has a separate maintenance, and acts and receives credit as a single woman. But see 4 *Durnf. & East*, 361, 766. 5 *Durn. & East*, 679. *Esp. Ca. Ni. Pri.* 6. Living apart

This, however, does not extend to the case of a woman eloping from her husband, and living apart from him. 2 *Black. Rep.* 1079. Eloping.

It may here be necessary to observe, that though a bill is drawn, indorsed, or accepted, by a person who cannot bind himself, it will nevertheless be valid against all those who are competent parties to the instrument. *Poth. pl.* 29.

Where the husband is under a civil disability of being in the kingdom; as where he is banished, or has abjured the realm, or has been transported, though but for a term of years; or where the husband is an alien enemy, residing out of the kingdom, a woman is considered as having an existence independent of her husband. *Co. Lit.* 132. *b.* 2 *Black. Rep.* 1197. *Salk.* 116. When the husband is banished, transported, &c.

A man may draw, accept, and indorse a bill by his agent, as well as by himself; and in these cases he is said to draw, accept, or indorse by procuration. As the doing either of these acts is the execution of a mere ministerial office, infants, *feme coverts*, persons attainted, outlawed, excommunicated May appoint an agent,

municated, aliens, and others incapable of contracting in
their own right, so as to bind themselves, may be agents
for these purposes. *Co. Lit.* 52. *a.*

by implica-tion.   And such authority may not only be express, but *implied*, and inferred from prior conduct of the principal:
it is therefore said, that if an agent has upon a former
occasion, in the principal's absence, usually accepted his
bills, and the principal on his return approved thereof,
it would bind him in a similar situation on a second absence
from home. It has also been decided, that a subsequent
assent will make the act of an agent binding on the
principal. *Mar* 2. *Ed.* 105. *Lord Raym.* 930. 3 *Durnf.
& East,* 757.

Caution is required in the choice of an agent.   As the principal will be bound by every act of his general
agent, even if he should exceed his authority; he
should be cautious whom he authorizes, as the consequences may be fatal to him; and if such agent leaves his
service he should acquaint his correspondents individually;
for till such information is communicated to those with
whom he has connections, an improper advantage may be
taken, as he will be bound by acts done subsequent to leaving his service, if done before the communication of such
intelligence.

CHAP. XI.

Of Bills of Exchange, &c. in cases of Bankruptcy.

Bankrupt's property vests in the assignees.   IF a man becomes a bankrupt, the property of bills
and notes of which he is the payee or indorsee, vests in his
assignees. And if in fact he indorse a bill and note after
his bankruptcy, and that be discovered before it is paid,
the assignees may recover it back from his indorsee in an
action of trover; and if the money be received, they may
recover the money in an action for so much money paid to
their use. *Beawes,* 469, 470.

But it has been adjudged, that if a trader delivers a bill
for a valuable consideration to another previous to an act of
bankruptcy, and forgets to indorse it, he may indorse it after
his bankruptcy. *Peake,* 50.

Payment

Payment to a person or his order, after knowing such person had committed an act of bankruptcy, would be inoperative. *Cooke's Bankrupt Laws.* 584, 5.

But a payment made to a bankrupt or his order, without notice of his being so, will in all cases discharge the person making it: and by a recent decision it appears, that if a debtor, after a secret act of bankruptcy of his creditor, gives him his acceptance in discharge of the debt, he may afterwards pay such acceptance to the holder of the bill; though after the acceptance, and before the bill became due, he heard of the drawer's bankruptcy: the giving, indorsing, or accepting a bill of exchange, being considered as an immediate payment, within the meaning of the statute of 1 *Jac.* 1. which protects *bona fide* pay-payments made to a bankrupt, provided the bill is honoured when due. 5 *Durnf.* & *East*, 711. Of paying after an act of bankruptcy.

And a payment made *by* a bankrupt to a person who had no notice of the bankruptcy, and being a *bone fide* creditor for goods sold, or by the bankrupt's having drawn, negotiated, or accepted a bill of exchange in the usual or ordinary course of trade and dealing, is protected by the statute 19 *G. II. c.* 32. which enacts, " that no person " who is or shall be really and *bona fide* a creditor of any " bankrupt, for or in respect of goods really and *bona* " *fide* sold to such bankrupt, or for or in respect of any " bill or bills of exchange really and *bona fide* drawn, " negotiated, or accepted by such bankrupt, in the usual " or ordinary course of trade and dealing, shall be liable to " refund or repay to the assignee or assignees of such " bankrupt's estate, any money which, before the suing " forth of such commission, was really and *bona fide*, and " in the usual and ordinary course of trade and dealing, " received by such person of any such bankrupt, before " such time as the person receiving the same shall know, " understand, or have notice that he is become a bank- " rupt, or that he is in insolvent circumstances." Where no notice has been given.

But this act, it is said, does not protect any payments but those expressly provided for; and therefore money paid by a trader after a secret act of bankruptcy to a carrier, for the carriage of goods, may be recovered by the assignees of the bankrupt. 5 *Durnf.* & *East*, 197. Exception.

And if the holder of a bill indulges the acceptor with time, on condition that he should allow interest, and he afterwards pays the bill, having first committed a secret Indulging with time.

4

act

act of bankruptcy, this is not payment in the course of trade within the meaning of the statute. 2 *Durnf. & Eaft.*

So also, where *A,* having recovered a verdict against *B.* who afterwards committed an act of bankruptcy, and *A.* not having had notice thereof, took a bill drawn by *B.* on *C.* for the amount of the sum recovered, payable at a distant period, which bill was afterwards paid; it was determined that this payment was not protected by the statute, and consequently that *A.* was liable to refund the money received by him to the assignees of *B.* 2 *H. B.* 334. *Chitty's Tr.* 154.

The holder of a bill not due may be a petitioning creditor. By the 7 *G. I. c.* 31, and 5 *G. II. c.* 30, the holder of a bill or notes whether due or not at the time of the bankruptcy, may, *if in poffeffion of the bill at the time,* either be petitioning creditor upon that account, or prove it under the commiffion; and even where it is not due, may receive a dividend of the bankrupt's eftate like other creditors, deducting intereft at the rate of 5*l. per cent.* only for the time the bill or note has to run: and the bankrupt in fuch cafe is exonerated from all future demand on account of fuch inftrument, if he obtains his certificate, as much as if it had been due before the act of bankruptcy. *Chitty's Tr.* 222.

Accommodation bill may be proved. Where a perfon has put his name to a bill or note to any amount, in order to accommodate another, and received a bill or note purporting to be to the fame amount, as a fecurity for having fo done, he may prove fuch bill or note, if in his poffeffion at the time of the bankruptcy, though he did not pay the accommodation bill till after the bankruptcy; the bill or note being a legal fecurity, creates an abfolute debt at law, and confequently gives a right to prove, though the holder may not have fuftained any damage at the time of fuch proof. *Cooke's Bank. Laws,* 159 7 *Durnf. & Eaft.* 366. *Efp.* 134.

Bill drawn before, and accepted after bankruptcy. When a bill or note is drawn before, but indorfed after the fecret act of bankruptcy of the acceptor to another perfon, the indorfee may be a petitioning creditor for the amount, or prove it under the commiffion, becaufe he ftands in the place of the perfon from whom he received fuch bill or note; and the debt is not created by the indorfement, but by the acceptance of the bill, or by making the note. *Cooke,* 19, 164. *Atk.* 72. 2 *Wilf.* 155.

                                             There

There is no doubt, and indeed it has been so decided, that if a person not having notice of the bankruptcy of the drawer, accepts a bill drawn on him after such bankruptcy, he will be justified in paying his acceptance, although he has afterwards heard of the bankruptcy. *7 Durnf. & East,* 711.

But he cannot set-off the amount of the sum payable, Set-off. to any demand on him by the assignees, because the statute 5 G. II. c. 30. relates only to mutual debts due before the bankruptcy. *Cooke,* 567. *Str.* 1234.

A debt at law, notwithstanding the statute of limita- Statute. tions has incurred, will support a commission; for the statute does not extinguish the debt, but the remedy, and the least hint will revive it. *2 Black. Rep.* 703.

Where the holder of a bill is entitled to prove, he may do so, not only under the commission against the acceptor, but also under that which has issued against the drawer or indorsers; and he may maintain an action against any party to the bill, who is solvent. *Cooke,* 168.

Where a person possessed of a bill or note, applies to Applying to prove it, *before* he has received a part of the sum engaged prove before for in the instrument, he may prove for the whole amount any part has been re- under all the commissions, and receive a dividend on his ceived. whole debt out of each estate, provided he does not receive more than 20s. in the pound upon it; though between such proof and the dividend, he may have received a part of the amount from a solvent or other party to the bill; but if the holder has received a part prior to his application to prove, he can only prove the remainder. *Cooke,* 151. 1 *Atk.* 107. 9. 2 *Vez.* 113.

If a person has discounted bills for another, who after-Bills dis- wards becomes bankrupt, and the holder proves the whole counted. amount of the bills: if any of the bills are afterwards paid in full, their amount must be deducted from the proof, and the future dividends are to be paid on the residue of the debt only. *Cooke,* 152.

Where bills have been given as a security for a general Collateral balance, or for a debt exceeding their amount, and upon security. a bankruptcy the creditor has proved his whole debt, excepting such bills; if any of them are duly honoured or paid, the sum received on them must be taken as a payment in part, and the future dividends made upon the residue of the debt. *Cooke,* 119, 120, 156.

The party holding an accommodation bill or note, as Holding an such instrument is for a valuable consideration, may prove accommoda- against tion bill.

I

againft all the parties but thofe from whom he received it, to the whole extent of it, and receive the dividends, provided they do not exceed 20s. in the pound on the confideration which he gave. *Cooke*, 157.

Of proving cofts and charges. The cofts and charges of protefting bills before an act of bankruptcy, may be proved; but not thofe which may have afterwards occurred; nor is the holder of a bill or note entitled to any intereft after the date of the commiffion iffued; nor, where the act of bankruptcy is afcertained, to any accrued after the bankruptcy: but the creditor may prove the whole fum for which the notes were given, notwithftanding he received a difcount at the rate of 5l. per cent. *Cooke*, 173. *Amb.* 172. 1 *Atk.* 140, 151. *Bailey's Sum.* 94.

On a queftion, whether the cofts and charges, incurred by protefting bills, after a commiffion of bankruptcy iffued, could be preved; Lord Hardwicke ordered that the cofts of the protefts arifen before the commiffion fhould be proved, but no part of the cofts arifen afterwards. 1 *Atk.* 140.

Debts bearing intereft. And *Ex parte Moore.* 2 *Bro. Cha. Cas.* 597. Previous to the 5th of May 1785, Mrs. Tyler accepted feveral bills drawn upon her by Moore, and on that day committed an act of bankruptcy, but no commiffion iffued until the 9th of March 1786; the bills became due between May 1785, and March 1786; and Mrs. Tyler not paying them, Moore did: he alfo paid 298l. for damages and charges, and the intereft amounted to 46l. 10s. The commiffioners permitted Moore to prove the fums for which the bills were drawn, but would not let him prove the intereft, or the fum paid for damages and charges; upon which he petitioned the Chancellor, but the Chancellor held that as the time when the act of bankruptcy was committed was afcertained, he could not carry the damages beyond that time; and the petition was difallowed.

Holder of a bill may fue affignees. A dividend of a bankrupt's eftate having been declared by the commiffioners, the holder of the bill may maintain an action againft the affignees for his fhare of the dividend, if they fhould refufe to pay him; and in fuch action the proceedings before the commiffion will be conclufive evidence of the debt; nor will the defendants, as affignees, be allowed to fet-off any debt due from the plaintiff to the bankrupt. *Brown v. Buller, Doug.* 407.

Drawing

Drawing and re-drawing bills of exchange, may, in certain cafes, be confidered as trading, fo as to render a party an object of the bankrupt laws. 1 *Atk.* 128. *Cowp.* 745.

The general rule, with refpect to debts carrying intereft, in cafe of bankruptcy, is that all intereft ceafes from the date of the commiffion; but if there be an eftate fufficient to pay 20s. in the pound, and a furplus, intereft fhall then revive, and be paid up to the final difcharge of the debt. 1 *Atk.* 79, 244.

Where the drawer or indorfer is a bankrupt at the time when acceptance or payment is refufed, it is not neceffary to give notice to him or his affignee; and it has been adjudged that the abfconding of the drawer will excufe the neglect to advife him. The fudden illnefs or death of the holder, or his agent, would alfo be an excufe for an omiffion of a regular notice to any of the parties, provided it is given as foon as poffible after the impediment is removed; but it is faid that the lofs of an accepted bill is no excufe. *Poth. pl.* 125, 144.

A queftion arifing on the validity of a commiffion of bankruptcy, on account of the infufficiency of the debt due to the petitioning creditor, the facts appeared to be thefe: the bankrupt being indebted to the petitioning creditors in the fum of 115l. 3s. 8d. on the 15th of September 1784, drew a bill for 80l. on the defendant (who till the time of the bankruptcy, and of the bill becoming due, was a creditor of the bankrupt) payable to the petitioning creditors, two months after date, and paid it to them on account of part of their debt: the bill was prefented for payment on the 18th of November following, and difhonoured. No notice however was ever given by the petitioning creditors to the bankrupt, or left at his houfe; a commiffion iffued againft the drawer on the 20th of November, on which he was declared a bankrupt in the afternoon of the 24th; that commiffion was afterwards fuperfeded, and another commiffion was iffued on the petition of the parties, on the amount of whofe debt the prefent queftion arofe. If the petitioning creditors, by not giving notice to the bankrupt of his bill being difhonoured, had made the bill their own, their debt was reduced within 100l. and then the commiffion could not be fupported; but if notice was not neceffary, the bill was not payment; their debt remained as it originally was, and the commiffion was valid. On the principles before ftated, the

I 2 court

court held that notice in this cafe was not neceffary, and therefore the commiffion was good. *Bickerdike v. Bollman,* 1 *Durnf. & Eaft,* 405.

A debt cannot be proved twice. According to what was faid by Lord Kenyon, C. J. in the cafe of Cowley and Dunlop, if the holder who has proved under the commiffion againft the acceptor, has received dividends on the bill, proportionably with the other creditors, an indorfer who has afterwards been compelled to pay the remainder of fuch bill, cannot come in and again prove the bill, becaufe the fame debt cannot be proved twice under the fame commiffion. 7 *Durnf. & Eaft,* 571, 2.

Where an indorfer has not proved before payment. If the holder whom an indorfer has been obliged to pay, has not proved before fuch payment, it feems doubtful whether the indorfer can afterwards come in under the commiffion. According to fome decifions he may, on the prefumption that the debt accrues by the acceptance; but in others it has been adjudged, that the payment being after the bankruptcy, the indorfer cannot prove; becaufe, by the payment of the bill he acquired a new caufe of action againft the acceptor, and at the time of the bankruptcy he had no demand againft him. This point has been feveral times litigated, but the laft cafe on this queftion is that of Cowley v. Dunlop, in which the court of King's Bench was equally divided. The judges were Mr. Juftice Lawrence, Mr. Juftice Grofe, Mr. Juftice Afhurft, and Lord Kenyon. *Cooke's Rule L.* 19, 165, 202, 269, 2 *H. B.* 640. *Cowp.* 525. *Str.* 1160. 3 *Wils.* 16. 7 *Durnford & Eaft,* 565.

CHAP. XII.

OF USURY RESPECTING BILLS, NOTES, &c.

Usury, what. USURY, in its original and ftrict fenfe, is a contract upon the loan of money, to give the lender a certain profit for the ufe of it at all events, whether the borrower made any advantage of it, or the lender fuffered any prejudice for the want of it; and in a more extenfive fenfe it feems, that all undue advantages taken by a lender againft a borrower, came under the notion of ufury. According to to the common law and feveral antient ftatutes; all ufury is unlawful; but, at this time, neither the common or ftatute law abfolutely forbid it. *Haw.* 245. 3 *Inft.* 151, 152.

Whatever were the prejudices of early times againft the taking of intereft, they appear to have been worn off in the reign of *Henry VIII*; a rational commerce having taught the nation that an eftate in money, as well as an eftate in land, houfes, and the like, might be let out to hire without the breach of one moral or religious duty. And, indeed, when the fource of this prejudice is examined, it will be found to have originated in a political, and not a moral precept; for though the Jews were prohibited from taking *ufury* [that is *intereft*] from their brethren, they were in exprefs words permitted to take it from a ftranger. 2 *Black.* 455, 456.

In the reign of *Henry VIII*, 10l. *per cent.* was allowed as the legal rate of intereft; but by 5 & 6 *Ed. VI. c.* 20. it was obferved that the ftatute 37 *Henry VIII, c.* 9, allowing this rate of intereft, had been conftrued to give a licence and fanction to all ufury not exceeding 10l. *per cent*; and this conftruction was declared to be utterly againft fcripture; and therefore all perfons were forbid to lend or forbear by any device for any *ufury, increafe, lucre,* or gain whatfoever, on pain of forfeiting the thing and the ufury or intereft, and of being imprifoned and fined.

And thus the law ftood till ftat. 13 *Eliz. c.* 8, which revived the ftatute of 37 *Henry VIII, c.* 9. and ordained that all brokers fhould be guilty of a *premunire* who tranfacted any contracts for more; and the fecurities themfelves fhould be void. By the 21 *Jac. I, c.* 17. the rate of intereft was reduced to 8l. *per cent.* and it having been lowered in 1650, during the ufurpation, to 6l. *per cent.* the fame reduction was re-enacted after the reftoration, by 12 C. II. c. 13. And laftly, the rate of intereft was reduced to 5l. *per cent.* by 12 *Anne, ft.* 2, c. 16.

The 12 *Anne, ft.* 2, c. 16, enacts, that no perfon, upon any contract which fhall be made, fhall take for the loan of any money, wares, &c. above the value of 5l. for the forbearance of 100l. for a year; and all bonds and *affurances* for payment of any money to be lent upon ufury, whereupon, or whereby there fhall be referved or taken above five pounds in the hundred, fhall be void; and every perfon

person which shall receive, by means of any corrupt bargain, loan, exchange, chevivance, shift or interest of any
wares or other things, or by any deceitful way, for forbearing or giving day of payment for one year, for their
money or other things, above 5l. for 100l. for a year, &c.
shall forfeit treble the value of the money or other things
lent.

Bill of ex-
change void
on an usuri-
ous contract.
If a bill of exchange or note is given, in consequence
of an usurious contract, it is absolutely void, when in the
hands of an innocent person, who may have taken it in
the fair and regular course of business, without any notice
of the usury: and evidence of usury will be a good defence
in an action brought upon such bill or note against the
drawer, acceptor, or indorser. *Doug.* 708. So in case
of gaming debts; the borrower may be a witness, though
the money is not paid, if the usury neither affects the debt,
nor avoids the contract: and where the matter is doubtful,
the objection shall only go to his credit, and not to his competency as a witness. 1 *Durnf. & East*, 153.

Premium.
If there is an agreement to pay legal interest, and a
premium is paid down over and above the interest, the
agreement is usurious and void.. 1 *Doug.* 235.

But the penalty is not incurred if the premium itself
does not exceed legal interest, nor till more than legal
interest is actually received. *Id.* An action may therefore be brought for the penalty, though more than a year
has elapsed since the payment of the premium, if it is
not a year since what has been paid exceeded legal interest. *Id.*

Where an
agreement
will admit
of a fair
construc-
tion.
E. 32 G. III, *Le Grand* v. *Hamilton*, a memorandum
indorsed on a bond, which was conditioned for the payment of 100l. by quarterly payments of 5l. each, and with
interest at 5l. per cent, "that at the end of each year,
the year's interest due was to be added to the principal,
and then the 20l. received in the course of the year was
to be deducted, and the balance remain as principal;"
was held not to be usurious, because the intention of the
parties might be to calculate the interest, at the end of the
year, in the following manner:—For the first quarter,
there would be interest on the whole sum; for the second,
interest for the whole, *minus* the sum already paid; and
so on for the third and fourth quarter; and whatever that
interest was, to be added to the principal. 4 *Durnf. &*
East, 613.

It

It is not usury for a country banker, in discounting bills, to take over and above 5*l.* discount, a commission, agreeable to the *usage,* on the amount of the bill   2 *Duraf. & East,* 52. Country banker may take commission.

But he must not take unreasonable advantages, as appears from the following case.   King's Bench, Guildhall, *Dec.* 18, 1793, *Matthews* v. *Griffith and Co.*   This was a *qui tam* action on the statute of usury.   The defendants are bankers at Portsmouth, and, in several instances, had discounted bills for a Mrs. *Stewart,* the proprietor of some silk works, at thirty days, at the rate of 5*l. per cent.* ; but, instead of giving cash, had given bills on London, at three days sight.   The fact was completely established by the evidence.   Mr. Erskine endeavoured to defend his clients, on the ground that it was by the consent of both parties, and for the convenience of Mrs. Stewart.   The objection was over-ruled by Lord Kenyon, who said he was confident it was usury, and no lawyer whatever would be of a different opinion.   They ought to have deducted the discount for their bills. But they must not take unreasonable advantages.

An agreement to pay double the sum borrowed, or other penalty on the non-payment of the principal debt at a certain day, is not usurious, because it is in the power of the borrower wholly to discharge himself, by repaying the principal according to the bargain.   1 *Haw.* 82.

So if a man lend another 100*l.* for two years, to pay for the loan 30*l.* but if he pay the principal at the year's end he shall pay nothing for the interest, this is not usury ; unless the clause of redemption be mere colour.   *Cro. Jac.* 509.   5 *Rep.* 69. Conditional loan.

The receipt of interest before the time when it is in strictness due, being voluntarily paid by the debtor, for the greater convenience of the creditor, or for any other such like consideration, without any manner of corrupt practice, or any previous agreement of this kind at the making of the first contract, does not make the party liable.   1 *Haw.* 82. Receiving interest before due.

The question of usury, or whether a contract is a colour and pretence for an usurious loan, or is a fair and honest transaction, must, under all its circumstances, be determined by a jury, subject to the direction of the court by a new trial.   See *Cowp.* 112, 770.   *Doug.* 708.   3 *Durnf. & East,* 351.

Where the bargain is merely casual, and the whole depends upon a contingency, the contract is not usurious ; but Where depending on a contingency.

but if the intereft *only* be hazarded on fuch a contract, and the principal is fecured, the whole is ufurious. *5 Bac. Abr.* 415. *Cro. Jac.* 508.

Refpecting foreign countries.

But if a contract, which carries intereft, be made in a foreign country, our courts will direct the payment of intereft according to the law of that country in which the contract was made. Thus *Irifh, American, Turkifh,* and *Indian* intereft have been allowed in our courts to the amount of 12*l. per cent.* For the moderation or exorbitance of intereft depends upon local circumftances; and the refufal to enforce fuch contracts would put a ftop to all foreign trade. *2 Black.* 463.

Contract voids the fecurity.

If a man gives a ufurious bond, and tenders the whole money, yet if the party will take only the legal intereft, he fhall not forfeit the treble value by the ftatute. *4 Leon.* 43. But though the treble value is not forfeited, unlefs fomething be *taken* above the legal rate; yet the contract *alone* voids the fecurity. *1 Haw.* 82. *Cro. Eliz.* 20.

Upon an information upon the ftatute of ufury, he who borrows the money may be a witnefs after he has paid the money. *1 Lord Raym.* 192. *2 Roll. Abr.* 685.

Intereft on money in Ireland, &c.

By 14 *G. III. c.* 79, all mortgages and other fecurities upon eftates and other property in Ireland, or the plantations, bearing intereft not exceeding 6*l. per cent.* fhall be legal, though executed in the kingdom of Great Britain, unlefs the money lent fhall be known at the time to exceed the value of the thing in pledge; in which cafe, alfo, to prevent ufurious contracts at home, under the colour of fuch foreign fecurities, the borrower fhall forfeit treble the fum fo borrowed.

Taking an advantage.

A contract referving to the lender a greater advantage than is allowed by the ftatute of ufury, is equally within the meaning of it; whether the whole be referved by way of intereft, or in part only under that name, and in part by way of rent for a houfe, let at a rate plainly exceeding the known value. *Cro. Jac.* 440.

Intention of the parties.

The conftruction of cafes of this nature, muft be governed by the circumftances of the whole matter, from which the intention of the parties will appear, in making the bargain; and if it was in truth ufurious, it is void, however it may be difguifed by a fpecious affurance. *1 Haw.* 82. *5 Rep.* 69.

Bankers may retain the difcount.

It may not be improper here to obferve that, in difcounting a bill or note, the difcount may be retained; for it has been adjudged, that intereft may be as lawfully
received

received before-hand for forbearing, as after the term is expired for having forborne: it fhould not therefore be reckoned merely as a loan of the balance, for in that cafe every banker in London, who takes 5*l. per cent* for difcounting bills, would be guilty of ufury: for if, upon difcounting a 100*l.* bill at 5*l. per cent.* he deducts the 5*l.* he may be conftrued to have lent only 95*l.* (that is, fuppofing the bill or note to have twelve months to run), and he has received intereft for five pounds more than the principal fum advanced, which is above the legal rate. But this doctrine feems only applicable to bills, promiffory notes, and other negotiable inftruments, and not to bonds. 2 *Bla. Rep.* 792. 3 *Ord on Ufury,* 54. 3 *Wilf.* 256, 262. *Chitty's Tr.* 54. An improper ufe might, however, be made of this indulgence (if fo it may be called), by iffuing bills or notes for large fums, to become due at a very diftant period; inftead of giving bonds, which, on account of the late additional ftamps, are now very expenfive; and thereby injuring the revenue, by holding out a colourable pretext for money-lenders to take fo apparent an advantage.

CHAP. XIII.

SUNDRY OBSERVATIONS AND DECISIONS RESPECTING BILLS OF EXCHANGE, &c.

BY the very act of drawing a bill, a perfon comes under an implied engagement to the payee, and to every fubfequent holder fairly entitled to the poffeffion, that the perfon on whom he draws is capable of binding himfelf by acceptance; that he is to be found at the place of which he is defcribed to be, if that defcription be mentioned in the bill; that if the bill be duly prefented to him, he will accept it in writing on the bill itfelf according to its tenor; and that he will pay it when it becomes due, if prefented, in proper time for that purpofe. *Kyd's Tr.* 109.

In default of any thefe particulars, the drawer is liable to an action at the fuit of any of the parties before-mentioned, on due diligence being exercifed on their parts, not only for the payment of the original fum mentioned in the

Engagement of the feveral parties.

Confequences of a default.

K   bill,

bill, but alſo in ſome caſes for damages, intereſt, and coſts : and he is equally anſwerable whether the bill was drawn upon his own account, or on that of a third perſon ; for the holder of the bill is not to be affected by the circumſtances that may exiſt between the drawer and another : the perſonal credit of the drawer being pledged for the honour of the bill. *Beawes*, 469.

A note or bill payable by inſtalments. Where a bill or note is payable by inſtalments, and it contains a clauſe that, on failure of payment of any one inſtalment the whole ſhall become due, the holder, on ſuch failure, can recover the whole amount of the ſum for which it was given ; but where there is not ſuch a clauſe in the inſtrument, it ſeems doubtful whether the holder can legally take a verdict for more than the inſtalment due. According to the caſe of Beckworth againſt Nott, and ſeveral other caſes cited by Lord Loughborough in that of *Rudder* v. *Price*, the plaintiff is entitled to the whole ſum for which the note was given ; but according to other caſes, and particularly that of *Aſhford* v. *Hand*, the plaintiff is only entitled to the inſtalments due at the time of commencing the action. Where, at the time of trial, nearly all the inſtalments are due, the jury will frequently give the whole ſum in damages, in order to avoid another action. If the plaintiff takes a verdict for more than the ſum remaining due, the court will either make him correct the verdict, and pay any expence the miſtake may have occaſioned, or grant a new trial. *Cro. Jac.* 505. 1 *H. B.* 551. 1 *H. B.* 88. *Cowp.* 571. *Bailey's Sum.* 90. *Chitty's Tr.* 213.

Taking a verdict for too much. *Pierſon* v. *Dunlop*. In an action againſt the acceptor upon a bill for 300l. the plaintiff took a verdict for the whole ſum ; the defendant filed a bill againſt him in the Exchequer, and he admitted in his anſwer that he had previouſly received 180l. from the drawer : this, among others, was urged as a ground for a new trial, and after cauſe ſhewn Lord Mansfield ſaid, " The verdict is certainly taken for 180l. more than was due ; there was no admiſſion of this payment at the trial, which was very wrong, and has been the occaſion of filing a bill in the Exchequer, therefore there ought to be a deduction of the money received, and a proportionable part of the intereſt, together with all the coſts in the Exchequer :" and though the court diſcharged the rule, they made the plaintiff remit the 180l. with intereſt upon it from the time it was paid, and pay the coſts of the bill and anſwer in the Exchequer. *Cowp.* 571.

Where

Where interest is expressed to be payable in the instrument itself, there cannot be a doubt of its being recoverable; and, as appears by several decisions, interest is generally payable on all liquidated sums from the time the principal is due: it is recoverable on bills and notes payable at a day certain, or after demand (if payable on demand), for money lent, and for money paid; but not for goods, sold, and work and labour. 3 *Wils.* 265. *Bla. Rep.* 761. *Burr.* 1077. 1 *H. B.* 305.

Where interest is expressed to be payable.

In some cases interest is said to be payable from the date of the note, as where it clearly appeared on the face of it to have been given for money lent; but, generally speaking, it carries interest only from the time of the demand of payment, unless the delay was occasioned by the defendant, as by his being absent from the kingdom, &c. when it was due; for interest being in the nature of damages for non-payment, the holder ought not to acquire a benefit by his own laches, and subject the drawer, acceptor, or indorser, to damages, when they are blameless. On this principle it appears to have been adjudged, that interest is only payable from the time the protest is made. A neglect to protest an inland bill for 20*l.* or upwards, will perhaps preclude the holder from recovering such interest or expences from persons entitled to notice of the non-acceptance or non-payment; but it will not preclude his recovering from any other person. *Prac. Reg.* 357. 6 *Mod.* 138. 10 *Mod.* 38. 2 *Bla. Com* 469. *Bailey's Sum.* 91. See *Stat.* 3. & 4. *Anne, f.* 9.

When to be reckoned from the date of the note.

In *Blaney v. Bradley*, the court held, that in actions upon promissory notes, payable on demand, interest should be given from the time of the demand proved; but in this case, where it appeared upon the face of the note to be for money *lent*, interest should be given from the date of the note. 9 *Mod.* 138.

The only expence the holder can be put to by the dishonour of a bill or note, is that of the charge for noting and protesting; and therefore he can demand no more of any of the parties to it than a satisfaction for that offence. But a party who has been obliged to pay the holder, in consequence of the acceptor's refusal, is frequently put to other expences by the return of the bill; such as re-exchange, postage, commission, and provision. Re-exchange is the expence incurred by the bill being dishonoured in a foreign country, where it was payable, and returned to that in which it was made or indorsed, and there taken up: the

amount

amount of it is regulated by the courſe of the exchange between the countries through which the bill has been negociated. 2 *Durnf.* & *Eaſt,* 52.

Dingwall v. *Dunſter. Douglas,* 235, 247. Dunſter accepted a bill merely to lend his credit, and to accommodate Wheate the drawer. *Fitzgerald,* the payee, indorſed it to Dingwall, and delivered it to him in payment for jewels. After it became due, the plaintiff, underſtanding that the acceptor never had any thing for it, and that Wheate was the real debtor, wrote to one *Ready, Wheate's* attorney, on the 6th of Eebruary, and, on the 4th of November 1775, preſſing him for the payment. Dunſter, on the 13th of February 1775, wrote a letter to Dingwall, thanking him in ſtrong terms for not proceeding againſt *him,* but mentioning in the ſame letter, that he had been informed by a perſon who had been ſent from him to Dingwall on the buſineſs, that Wheate had taken up the bill, and given another to Dingwall's ſatisfaction. It did not appear that Dingwall took any notice of that letter. But he for ſome time received intereſt on the bill from Wheate, and alſo the principal due by another bill, made at the ſame time, and drawn and accepted by the ſame parties, and under the like circumſtances. The plaintiff ſuffered ſeveral years to elapſe without calling on Dunſter, or treating him as his debtor. The queſtion was, whether the plaintiff, by his conduct, had diſcharged the acceptor; and the court unanimouſly held that he had done nothing from which it could be concluded he meant to abandon his claim againſt him. He had done right in applying to Wheate for payment, as he was appriſed that he was in fact the debtor, and Dunſter was ſo far ſenſible of his kindneſs as to thank him for his indulgence in a letter: had the ſuggeſtion in that letter been true, relative to the plaintiff's having delivered up the bill to Wheate, that might have made a material difference; but the plaintiff having returned no anſwer to the letter, and the fact not having been attempted to be proved at the trial, it is probable the aſſertion was not warranted.

De Bert v. *Atkinſon.* In an action againſt the payee of a note, it appeared that the note was not preſented for payment till the day after it became due, and that no notice was given to the defendant till five days after ſuch preſentment; but it alſo appearing that the defendant gave no value for the note, that he lent his name merely to give it credit, and that he knew at the time that the maker

was

was infolvent, *Eyre*, C. J. directed the jury to find for the plaintiff, which they did. A rule to fhew caufe why there fhould not be a new trial was afterwards granted, and upon caufe fhewn, per *Eyre*. C. J. " If the maker is not known to be infolvent, infolvency will not excufe the want of an early demand ; but knowledge excludes all prefump- tion which could otherwife arife ; here the money was to be raifed upon the defendant's credit ; he meant to gua- rantee the payment, and no lofs could happen to him from the want of notice." And per *Buller*, J. " The general rule is only applicable to fair tranfactions. Where the bill or note has been given for value in the ordinary courfe of trade, it is faid infolvency does not take away the neceffity of notice ; that is true where value has been given, but no further ; here the defendent lent his name merely to give credit to the note, and was not an indorfer in the common courfe of bufinefs." *Heath* and *Rooke*, Js. concurring, the rule was difcharged. 2 *H. B.* 336.

In *Corney* v. *Da Cofta* and Co.—*Efpinaffe*, 302. Da Cofta and Co. compounded with their creditors, and to fecure the compofition drew notes in favour of the defend- ant, which he indorfed to the creditors. The defendant took effects of Da Cofta and Co. at the time, to the amount of the compofition ; and an action being brought againft him upon one of thefe indorfements, he infifted that he had no notice of the non-payment of the note until five weeks after it was due ; but *Buller*, J. held he was not entitled to notice, and the plaintiff had a verdict. *[margin: Where not entitled to notice.]*

But in *Staples* v. *Okines*—*Efpinaffe*, 332. In an action againft the drawer of a bill, the defence was want of notice ; the plaintiff thereupon called the acceptor, who proved that when the bill was drawn he was indebted to the de- fendant in more than the amount of the bill, but that he then reprefented to the defendant that it would not be in his power to provide for the bill when it fhould become due, and that it was therefore then underftood between them that the defendant fhould provide for it, and it was contended that this fuperfeded the neceffity of giving the defendant notice ; but Lord *Kenyon* held it did not, and non-fuited the plaintiff. *[margin: Where no- tice is ne- ceffary.]*

Though it is faid a very fmall matter will amount to an acceptance, and that any words which do not put a nega- tive on the requeft will be fufficient ; yet fee the cafe of *Powel* v. *Jones, Efpinaffe* 17. In an action againft the defendant as acceptor of a bill, the only evidence to prove the acceptance was, that when the bill was called for he *[margin: What is not an accept- ance.]*

returned

returned it, and ſaid, " There is your bill, it is all right."
Lord *Kenyon* thought theſe words could by no implica-
cation amount to an acceptance, and non-ſuited the plaintiff.

Maſon v. *Hunt*—*Doug* 284, 297. Rowland Hunt, in
Dominica, agreed with a houſe there that his partner Thomas Hunt, in London, ſhould in conſequence of a cargo,
of tobacco being conſigned to him, with the bills of lading, and an order for inſurance, accept ſuch bills as that
houſe ſhould draw on him at the rate of 80*l*. per hogſhead:
inſurance for the ſum of 3600*l*. was ordered on forty hogſheads of tobacco, which Thomas Hunt procured for a
premium of 303*l*. Bills were afterwards drawn on him
for 3200*l*. payable to one of the partners of the houſe, on
account of forty hogſheads of tobacco, and indorſed by
Rowland Hunt to Maſon. The bills arrived and were
preſented for acceptance. Thomas Hunt refuſed to accept them, ſuppoſing the tobacco was not worth the money
at which it was rated. After a negotiation of ſome days,
Maſon took the bill of lading, and the policy of inſurance
out of the hands of Thomas Hunt. When the tobacco
arrived, it was ſold by the plaintiff Maſon, and produced
no more than 1400*l*. Under the direction of Lord Mansfield, a verdict was given for the defendant, and on an
application for a new trial, his lordſhip ſaid.—An agreement to accept may in many inſtances, amount to an acceptance: but an agreement is ſtill but an agreement,
and if it be conditional, and a third perſon, knowing of
the conditions annexed to the agreement, take the bill, he
takes it ſubject to ſuch agreement. Here were ſeveral
things ſpecified as the conditions of the acceptance—
the number of hogſheads to be delivered—of a certain value rated by the hogſhead—the inſurance—the
bills of lading—the conſignment. On the face of
the agreement, I thought at the trial, and ſtill incline
to think, that the meaning of the parties was, that tobacco ſhould be conſigned which would be worth 80*l*.
per hogſhead: this fell immenſely ſhort of that value. It
is plain the *Hunts* never *meant* to be in advance, and I
think ſo great a difference in the value ſuch a fraud as to
entitle the defendants to relief *againſt the agreement*. But
as to this the reſt of the court have doubted, becauſe there
is no evidence to ſhow how the decreaſe in the value aroſe.
But the reſt of the court are extremely clear that the ſubſequent conduct of the plaintiff makes an end of the whole,
and I think the reaſons are unanſwerable. That part of
the

Marginal note: Conditional acceptance depends upon circum- ſtances.

the cafe ftands thus. The Hunts fay, " we are not bound: this is an impofition: the tobacco is of inferior value. The letter reprefents it as worth 80*l.* the infurance makes it 90*l.* per hogfhead; and it turns out not to be worth 40*l.*" If Mafon had meant to fay, " you are liable, and fhall pay the bills," what would his conduct have been? He would have left the policy of infurance and the bills of lading in their hands, and fued them upon the acceptance. The temptation to accept was the commiffion on the af-fignment, and they were to have the fecurity of the goods and the infurance. But the plaintiff undoes all this, and fays, then I will take all from you, fecurity, commiffion, &c. This was faying, " I will ftand in your place, but not fo as to be anfwerable for more than the produce of the tobacco." It is impoffible the defendants could mean to accept, without any benefit or fecurity. We are all clear that this made an end of the agreement. *Kyd's Tr.* 162.

If the holder of a bill of exchange brings feparate ac-tions againft the acceptor, the drawer, and indorfers, at the fame time, the court will ftay the proceedings in any ftage of the action againft the drawer, or any one of the indor-fers, upon payment of the amount of the bill, and the cofts of that particular action; but the action againft the acceptor will only be ftayed on the terms of his paying the cofts in all the actions, he being the original defaulter. 4 *Durnf. & Eaft,* 691. *Str.* 515. See *Bla. Rep.* 749.

(Of bringing feparate actions againft the parties.)

Where a note is given by two, to pay jointly *or* fever-ally, the payee may fue both or either; if he fue both, he may declare on the note in the words of it jointly *or* fever-ally; but if he fue either of them fingly, it was formerly held that he could not declare in that way, but that he muft ftate the note as given only by one; and that the joint *or* feveral note would be good evidence to fupport fuch a declaration. *Str.* 76. 2 *Lord Raym.* 1544. 2 *Str.* 819.

(Note payable jointly or feverally.)

But it is now held, that in an action on a joint or fepa-rate promiffory note againft one, a declaration that he and another made their promiffory note, by which they *jointly and feverally* promifed to pay, is good; for if *or* muft be underftood as a disjunctive, the election whether the note fhall be joint or feveral, is in the perfon to whom it is given, and by fuing one, he fhews his election to confider it as a feveral note; but in this cafe the true conftruction of the word *or* is, that it is fynonimous with *and.* They both

(How to be ftated in the declaration.)

both promiſe that *they* or *one of them* ſhall pay; therefore the liability is on *both*, and on each. The nature of the tranſaction demands this conſtruction. *Rees* v. *Abbot, Cowp.* 832. *Kyd's Tr.* 186.

And per *Buller*, J. If the note had been jointly only, and it had been ſtated as a ſeveral one, no advantage could have been taken of this but by a plea in abatement.

Of reindor-
ſing.

A perſon who has indorſed a bill or note cannot, in general, maintain an action on a re-indorſement to him, againſt the party to whom he indorſed. In *Biſhop* v. *Hayward*, 4 *Durnf. & Eaſt.* 470. Biſhop declared on a promiſſory note made by *Collins* payable to Biſhop or order, and afterwards indorſed by him to the defendant Hayward, who afterwards re-indorſed it to Biſhop. On the general iſſue a verdict was given for the plaintiff: a motion was made in arreſt of judgment, on the ground that there was no cauſe of action ſtated on the record. The court ſaid, that the conſequence of ſupporting this verdict would be, that the plaintiff, without having any real demand on the defendant, might recover againſt him by the judgment of the court, without allowing the defendant a poſſibility of defending himſelf; that on the trial it was only neceſſary for him to prove that the note in queſtion was given, as ſtated in the declaration, payable to the plaintiff; that it was indorſed by him to the defendant, and re-indorſed by the latter to the plaintiff. The defendant could not deny theſe facts, and on proving them he had proved his whole declaration, and therefore entitled to a verdict. But the court were bound to ſee whether, on this ſtatement of the caſe, the plaintiff had ſhewn ſufficient to entitle him to judgment. There might be circumſtances which, if diſcloſed on the record, might entitle the plaintiff to recover againſt the defendant on this note, as if he had ſtated that his own name was originally uſed for form only; and that it was underſtood by all the parties, that the note, though nominally made payable to the plaintiff, was in reallity to be paid to the defendant; but then the note ſhould have been declared on according to its legal import. Here nothing appeared but that the plaintiff, being the original indorſer of the note, called on the defendant, who appeared upon the record to be a ſubſequent indorſee. Nothing could be clearer in law than that an indorſee might reſort to any of the preceding indorſers for payment; but the preſent action was an attempt to reverſe this rule. The court could,
in

in this cafe, prefume nothing but what was ftated in the
record; the cafes where prefumption was admitted were
where the plaintiff ftated a title defective in form, not
were he had fhewn a title defective in itfelf, which was the
cafe here.

The original contract on negotiable bills and notes is
to pay to fuch perfon as the payee or his indorfees fhall
direct. When the payee affigns it over, he does it by the
law of merchants; for being a *chofe in action*, it is not
affignable by the general law. The indorfement is part of
the original contract, as incidental to it, and muft be underftood to be made in the fame manner as the inftrument
was drawn: the indorfee holds it in the fame manner, and
with the fame privileges and powers as the original payee,
as a transferable inftrument, which he may indorfe over to
another, and that other to a third, &c. 2 *Burr.* 1226.

Hence it has been often folemnly fettled, that it is no objection to the claim of an indorfee, that the indorfement to
him does not contain the words "to order."

In one cafe, viz. that of *More* v. *Manning, Com.* 311,
it appeared that Manning had given a promiffory note to
Statham or order; Statham indorfed it to Wetherhead,
but did not add, "or to his order," and Wetherhead indorfed it to the plaintiff, who, on non-payment at the time,
brought an action againft Manning. The defendant contended, that as there were no exprefs words to authorife
Wetherhead to affign it, he had no fuch power; but the
whole court refolved, that as the bill was at firft affignable
by Statham, as being payable to him or order, and as all
Statham's intereft was transferred to Wetherhead, the right
of affigning it was transferred alfo, and the plaintiff had
judgment.

In the cafe of *Achefon* v. *Fountain*, the plaintiff had declared on an indorfement made by *William Abercrombie,*
by which he appointed the payment to be to *Louifa Achefon,* "or order." On producing the bill in evidence, it
appeared to be originally made payable to Abercrombie or
order; but Abercrombie's indorfement was in thefe words
—"Pray pay the contents to *Louifa Achefon.*" It
was objected that the indorfement did not agree with the
declaration. This being ftated in the declaration as an
indorfement to Achefon, or order, it was objected that it
was a fatal variance. The court, however, gave judgment, on the ground of a general propofition in law, that a
bill is negotiable without the addition of thefe words to

L   the

the indorfement; the legal import of fuch indorfement being, that the bill was payable to order, and that the plaintiff might on this have indorfed it over to another, who would have been the proper order of the firft indorfer. *Str.* 457. *Bull. Ni. Pri.* 275.

The words, or order, originally omitted, but fupplied by another. The fame point was again agitated on the following occafion. *Edie* v. *Eaſt India Company*—Colonel Clive drew a bill, payable to Mr. Campbell, or order, on the Eaſt India Company, who accepted it. Mr. Campbell indorfed it to Mr. *Robert Ogilby*, but the words, "or order," being originally omitted, were inferted by another hand before the trial. Ogilby indorfed it over to Meſſrs. *Edie* and *Laird*, or order, and afterwards, before the payment, became infolvent. *Edie* and *Laird* brought an action againſt the Company as acceptors, who refuſed payment, alledging that Ogilby had no right to aſſign to the plaintiffs. At the trial, Lord Mansfield permitted the defendants to give evidence of a *uſage among merchants*, and the jury found for the defendants. On application for a new trial, the counfel in fupport of the verdict refted principally on the ufage which had been eſtabliſhed by the evidence; and with refpect to the two cafes of *More* v. *Manning*, and *Acheſon* v. *Fountain*, they endeavoured to ſhew that they did not apply to this; the firſt, they faid, muſt have been an indorfement in blank, not to Wetherhead by name, and then his power to transfer it could not be doubted: and with refpect to the fecond, that did not decide the prefent queſtion, for it was only an objection on account of the declaration varying from the evidence: the plaintiff had clearly a right to recover, without entering into the general queſtion, for ſhe was the perſon to whom the bill was indorfed, and had not indorfed it over; and what the court was reported to have faid, "as to her power to have indorfed it to another, who would be the proper order of the firſt indorfer," was at leaſt extrajudicial, if not added by the reporter himſelf. But the court, on full deliberation, were of opinion, that the law was fettled by thoſe two cafes, that fuch an indorfement was good, and gave the indorfee a right of indorfing over: that the law having been fo fettled, no evidence of an ufage to it ought to have been admitted; that the law of merchants is the law of the kingdom, and part of the common law, and when once eſtabliſhed by judicial determinations, cannot be ſhaken. Where indeed the law of merchants is doubtful, the evidence of a cuſtom may be received; but even then it muſt be

be proved by facts, not by opinion only, and must be consistent with the general principles of the law. 1 *Black.
Rep.* 295. *Burr.* 1216. *Kyd's Tr.* 98.

Yet an indorsement may be restrictive, and then it ope-
rates to preclude the person to whom it is made from trans-
ferring the instrument to another, so as to give him a right
of action, either against the person imposing the restriction,
or against any of the preceding parties. *See* page 25. of this
work.

We have been very particular in stating the following
recent case, as the circumstances and decision are of the
very last importance to the public.

July 16, 1801. Sittings before Lord *Kenyon* and a
special jury; *Lawson*, baronet, and others, *v. Weston* and
others. The leading counsel for the plaintiff stated, that
the plaintiffs in this case were persons of the highest respectability and honour, constituting the Richmond Bank
in Yorkshire, and brought this action against the defendants, very respectable persons likewise, and constituting the
firm of the Southwark Bank. The defence of this action
was no reflection on the defendants, inasmuch as they were
merely nominal defendants, and were indemnified by the
person actually interested. In Westminster-hall, in Guildhall, and in the city of London, it was supposed, the question that was now to be raised, had been at rest since 1764,
when the case of *Grant* and *Vaughan* was decided, and is
reported in 3 *Burr.* 1516. This is precisely the same case,
without the possibility of being able to distinguish it. It
was an action brought on a bill of exchange for 500*l.* by
the plaintiffs, as indorsees, against the defendants, as acceptors. It would be lamentable in these times, as it had
been justly observed by high authority, when we *eat and
drink paper*, and *live upon paper*, if the plaintiffs were not
entitled, in this case, to recover. The bill was drawn by
Mr. *Vasy*, at fifty days, on the defendant, who accepted in
favour of a *Thomas Stokes*, who indorsed it to a *William
Spiers*, who had the bill stolen from him. It then passed
into the hands of a person who described himself as *J. Warren*; who took the paper in the ordinary way to the shop of
the plaintiffs, in Richmond, and desired to have it discounted. The confidential agent of this Bank, knowing Mr.
Vasy perfectly well, who lived in the neighbourhood, and
he also knowing the respectability of the defendants, the
acceptors, and seeing the bill regularly indorsed, did not
hesitate to discount it. He was perfectly aware that the

Respecting country Banks.

L 2 persons

perfons who brought this action againft the acceptors, muft be in a condition to fhew they had paid a full and valuable confideration for it. The cafe of *Grant* and *Vaughan* was decided againft him. It was faid in that cafe, if it were decided in favour of the plaintiff, a perfon who found or ftole a bill might bring an action upon it. "No (faid Lord *Mansfield*), becaufe the perfon who brought the action muft fhew that it came to him fairly." He fhould prove that the prefent plaintiffs paid a full confideration for it, and difcounted it juft as the Bank of England, or any private banker, would have done. He faid he ought to make an apology to his Lordfhip, and the gentlemen of the jury, for having wafted a minute of their time in ftating it. The bill was dated March 30, 1801, drawn in favour of Mr. Stokes, and indorfed by him to Thomas Spiers, from whom this bill had been ftolen. Lord *Mansfield*, in the cafe of *Grant* and *Vaughan*, faid, if one of the two perfons had been guilty of negligence, and the queftion was, which of them fhould bear the lofs, the anfwer was clear; he who had been guilty of negligence. Mr. Spiers, the holder of the bill, ought not to have indorfed it till he had been going to pay it away. If he had kept it unindorfed in his poffeffion, it would have been perfectly fafe.

The bill was read. It was dated March 30, 1801. "Fifty days after date, pay to the order of Mr. Thomas Stokes 500*l.* value received. *William Vafy.*" Accepted by the defendants, and indorfed *Thomas Stokes, William Spiers,* and *J. Warren.* The hand-writing of the parties was admitted. This was the plaintiff's cafe.

Mr. *Attorney General,* for the defendants, faid, they had not proved they had paid value for it.

Lord *Kenyon* faid, it was a very good *prima facie* cafe.

The leading counfel for the defendants faid, he did not rife to difpute any of the general propofitions laid down by his learned friend. He admitted that a bill of exchange drawn, indorfed, and accepted, might be negotiated, and that any holder of fuch bill, *bona fide,* for a valuable confideration, might maintain an action upon it, although in the courfe of coming to him, it might be acquired by fraud, or even by theft, which was eftablifhed in the cafe of *Miller* and *Race.* But, he contended here, that unlefs a bill of exchange came in the fair and ordinary courfe of trade—unlefs it came without circumftances that indicated any fufpicion—the holder was not entitled to recover. This

4   bill

bill was offered to be difcounted at the Richmond Bank, under fingular circumftances. After it had been accepted in London, at a confiderable diftance of time after it was drawn and accepted, and within three weeks of its becoming due, it was prefented at the Richmond Bank; and that impofed on them that degree of attention, and that duty which was neceffary to avoid impofition; and which duty was exercifed by other perfons when a bill of fo large an amount was prefented by a man who was a total ftranger. The Richmond Bank chofe to difcount it, by giving 250*l.* in fmall notes of their own, and a bill for the other 250*l.* payable on their agents in London. Now, it had been decided, that fuch bill of exchange muft appear to have been taken fairly and *bona fide* in the courfe of trade, and with the greateft caution and prudence. That was a duty which every man, in negotiating bills of exchange, had a right to expect at the hands of another. Did there not exift in this cafe many circumftances to impofe the duty of inquiry? He would fhew, by witneffes, that it was an extremely unufual thing, and he did not believe they could fhew a fingle inftance of a bill of the magnitude of 500*l.* having been accepted in London, and, in the regular courfe of circulation, getting back again to Yorkfhire, and then difcounted without a fingle queftion afked. If thefe things were to be done—if one man did not lend another the affiftance of his prudence and caution—impofitions of this fort would be endlefs. It was advertifed feveral times in three or four of the London papers, in the moft extenfive circulation, that fuch a bill was miffing, and defiring the perfons, into whofe hands it might come, to ftop it. This bill had been drawn by a Mr. *Vafy*, who is a gentleman in the neighbourhood of Newcaftle, on his bankers in town, in favour of Mr. *Stokes*, his agent, who had paid it to Mr. *Spiers*, who carrying it to be difcounted, it was ftolen from him. It was fome time before it became due—they had notice, and they might have ftopped their own bill for 250*l.* They took no means of that fort, but conducted themfelves with a culpable degree of negligence.

Lord Kenyon. What do you fay is the amount of a bill that ought to pafs, as coming from a ftranger?

The counfel fuppofed a bill for 10,000*l.* to be brought to any bank by a ftranger—Was it for a banker immediately to fill his pocket with his own fhop notes, or ought not rather the magnitude of the fum to have ftaggered him?

him ? He should prove, by bankers, that they would not have discounted it without making inquiry. But what was the best proof, they had done so, and not receiving satisfaction, the bill was returned. He should prove that such a bill circulating in the country, must necessarily excite suspicion, and that they would have paused on such a bill, and would not have discounted it in the manner the plaintiffs had done. They made no inquiry—they did not ask a single question—but discounted the bill at once, from the avidity, which was extremely culpable in them, of getting into circulation a vast quantity of their own paper, which was productive of mischief, and which he really thought required some public check. In prudence and justice they ought not to have discounted it. The decision in the case of *Peacock* and *Rhodes* had established that some degree of caution ought to be used, in discounting bills to a man accredited in no shape whatever.

Lord Kenyon observed, that when a bill of the magnitude of 500*l.* was used as an argument, he dreaded that argument that rested solely on the amount of the bill. He admitted such expressions were used by great authorities; but when he found this exception, he doubted there was some little malady in the argument. When this bill was presented at the Richmond Bank, ought they to have taken a horse and come up to London to inquire of the acceptors? Some drafts to a very large amount were brought to town, by tenants to some great men, ought they to be sent back to the country to trace the different hands through which such drafts had passed? A noble Duke, to whom the country was as much indebted as any other man in it for the improvements he had made [*meaning the Duke of Bridgewater*] drew a draft for 100,000*l.* in favour of the public.

The counsel for the defendant said, as it had come through the regular channel of that noble Duke, no person could suspect it.

Lord Kenyon said, if he could shew any blameable negligence in the Richmond Bank, he would do something: but here was a bill accepted by a respectable house, circulating through the country, and got into the hands of a Mr. *Warten,* who unfortunately turned out to be a male Miss *Robertson.* I cannot tell, said his Lordship, what to do with it—it would paralyze the whole trade of the country. I am not sure if this defence was to be admitted, that it would not go to bills of 10*l.* and there would

be

be a total end of all paper credit. Unlefs the jury infer culpable negligence in the plaintiffs or their agents, I do not know how the acceptors can defend themfelves againft the payment of this bill. With refpect to the advertifement of this bill, in a number of the London newfpapers, I know from experience that fuch meafures may have been taken, and yet fuch papers have not reached the parties in the country. If it had appeared that it had been inferted in a paper that circulated in that part of the country, that perhaps might have been a degree of evidence. I remember when I was a counfel at the bar, an action brought in the county of Hereford to recover ten guineas. A reward to that amount had been advertifed in a newfpaper that was circulated in that county, to any perfon who would produce a horfe that had been ftolen. The advertifement was figned by the defendant, and the horfe was found by the plaintiff, and reftored. The defendant denied that he knew any thing of the advertifement. An action was brought, and the ten guineas recovered, on the ground that, as the paper was read in that county, the jury inferred he muft have known of the advertifement.

Robert Wilkinfon, a witnefs, faid he was partner in a banking houfe with Mr. *Lumley*, at *Stockton*, and was applied to, to difcount this bill. He knew the drawer. The perfon who brought it was not a well dreffed man. It was their courfe never to difcount bills that were brought by ftrangers. He not only fpoke of his own mode of dealing, but he had never heard of any inftance of its being done before in the north.

Lord Kenyon afked how far north it went—whether it was only to the Trent, or on the other fide of it?

The witnefs did not anfwer to that queftion; but, on a crofs examination, faid, he had come up to London for the purpofe of this caufe. The perfon who offered the bill to be difcounted, from his appearance, excited his fufpicion. He could not conceive how a perfon of his appearance, could be honeftly in poffeffion of a bill to that amount.

Mr. *Lightly* (clerk of the Northallerton bank) faid, he recollected a perfon offering the bill in queftion to be difcounted. He did not difcount it becaufe he did not know the man. The perfon who offered the bill, was a man of very genteel appearance and good addrefs.

Lord

Lord Kenyon here obſerved, that the other witneſs would not diſcount it becauſe the perſon who brought it had not the appearance of a gentleman, and had no addreſs.

The witneſs farther ſaid, that he ſeemed to be a very well informed man. He was a total ſtranger to him. They frequently diſcounted bills for ſtrangers; but he never recollected a bill to ſuch an amount preſented by a ſtranger, before that, to be diſcounted.

Lord Kenyon remarked, that ſome country banks only diſcounted bank bills, for the circulation of their own paper. Men might lay down a particular rule to themſelves. Some were more ſcrupulous than others; and if the defendants could throw the leaſt ſuſpicion on the conduct of the plaintiffs, or of their not paying a valuable conſideration for this bill, he ſhould liſten to it with both his ears. There might be ſome conveniencies attending theſe banks, but there were alſo ſome inconveniencies; and they ought to be under ſome other regulations. His Lordſhip farther obſerved, that there are advertiſements in ſeveral newſpapers, which circulate in Derbyſhire, Nottinghamſhire, and other counties of England, ſtating that banks are to be opened in quarters—to ſay no more.——— I am very much alarmed for ſeveral great towns, where ſome perſons are going to open banking ſhops—perſons who, in London, where they are known, would not be truſted with one farthing.

Mr. *Smart* ſaid he was a banker in London, and it was not the cuſtom here to diſcount bills to a large amount for ſtrangers.

Mr. *Gibbs* obſerved that this was dangerous evidence.

Lord Kenyon ſaid there was no danger of informing a jury of merchants at Guildhall as to what is uſual for bankers in London to do.

Mr. *Barnewell* ſaid, that bankers in town commonly diſcounted bills only for their cuſtomers who kept accounts with them.

Lord Kenyon remarked, that he did not think what the witneſs ſaid was evidence. According to that you muſt take the gauge of every man's judgement, which would lead into a ſea of uncertainty.

The counſel ſaid, he wiſhed to ſhew the courſe of the trade.

Lord Kenyon replied, that the courſe of trade depended

upon

upon the convenience of every man. He did not know where they would go. They would have no rule upon earth.

Mr. *Vaux* faid, he believed it was very well known that there was not the fmalleft analogy between a banker in London, and in the country.

The defendant's counfel obferved, that the country bankers, who ought to exercife a greater degree of caution than bankers in London, ufed much lefs, from the defire they had of circulating their own paper.

Mr. *Prieftman*, who was clerk to the plaintiffs, was called upon to prove that they had paid a full and valuable confideration for the bill in queftion. He difcounted the bill—he knew the drawer Mr. *Vafy*—he had repeatedly difcounted his bills before to a large amount. He gave a full and valuable confideration for the bill in queftion; he alfo knew Stokes's hand-writing; and a Mr. Stapleton, who was in their houfe at the time, knew the hand-writing of the defendants.

On crofs examination, he faid, he paid it by a bill on London for 250*l*. and the reft in fmall notes. The perfon who brought the bill faid his name was *Warren*. He had a refpectable appearance: he feemed to be about fixty, and looked as if he meant to refide in the country. He had fo much the appearance of a gentleman, that he made the draft payable to John Warren, Efq. He faid he had never difcounted a bill to fo large an amount before to a ftranger.

When the counfel for the defendant was afking this gentleman why he had not been more particular in his inquiries, and afked this man where he lived, &c.

Lord Kenyon afked the counfel what he would have faid if any cafhier of a country bank had afked him thefe queftions? His Lordfhip faid fuch queftions went to the circulation of every bank note that had been iffued.— " How came you by fuch a note? It is not likely that a man, with fuch a coat, fhould be honeftly in poffeffion of fuch a note;—of a note to fo large an amount."

The defendant's counfel obferved, that in one of the cafes which had been decided on this fubject, fufpicions refted upon the man that offered the note, becaufe he had a round hat, and a great coat, and therefore was taken for a highwayman. But now, from the general drefs of the country, according to thefe marks, every man was a highwayman.

M   *Lord*

Lord Kenyon obferved, if they could not impute any thing to raife a fair fufpicion againft the conduct of the plaintiffs, they had made out their cafe. Verdict for the plaintiffs, 500l.

For the fatifaction of our readers, we fhall ftate the cafe of *Grant* and *Vaughan*, as mentioned in 3 *Burr.* and referred to in the above decifion.

Poffeffor for a valuable confideration entitled to payment.

Grant v. *Vaughan*, 3 *Burr.* 1516. 1 *Bl. Rep.* 485. *Vaughan*, a merchant in London, gave to Bickwell, one of his fhips hufbands, a draft on his banker Sir Charles Afgill, payable to fhip Fortune, or bearer. Bicknell loft the draft; the perfon who found it, or at leaft was in poffeffion of it, went four days after the note was payable, to the fhop of *Grant*, a tradefman at Portfmouth, and having bought fome tea gave him the note in payment, and defired to have the balance. *Grant* ftepped out to make inquiry who Vaughan might be, and being informed he was a refponfible man, and that the note was in his hand-writing, gave the change out of the note, retaining the price of the tea. *Vaughan* being apprifed that Bicknell had loft the note, fent notice to Sir *Charles Afgill* not to pay it. Payment being accordingly refufed, Grant brought his action againft *Vaughan* as the drawer. The caufe was tried by a fpecial jury of merchants, who found for the defendant. On an application for a new trial, the court held that thefe notes were transferable by mere delivery; and however the true owner may have loft them, the fair poffeffor, for a valuable confideration, was entitled to the money. See alfo *Kyd's Tr.* 103.

Though the note has been ftolen.

And in the cafe of *Miller* v. *Race*, alfo referred to in *Lawfon* v. *Wefton*. A bank note, payable to *William Finney*, or bearer, was ftolen out of the mail in the night of the 11th of December 1756, and on the 12th came to the hands of the plaintiff, for a full and valuable confideration, in the ufual courfe of bufinefs, and without any knowledge that it had been taken out of the mail. He afterwards prefented it at the bank for payment; and the defendant, being one of the clerks, ftopped it, upon which an action of trover was brought: and upon a cafe referved upon the point, whether the plaintiff had a fufficient property in the note to entitle him to recover, the court was clear in opinion that he had, and that the action was well brought. *Burr.* 451.

CHAP.

CHAP. XIV.

STAMPS REQUIRED ON BILLS OF EXCHANGE, PRO-
MISSORY NOTES, DRAFTS, OR ORDERS.

BY the 31 G. III. c. 25. and the 37 G. III. c. 90. the
following duties are payable on the above-mentioned in-
struments.

Bills, Notes, Drafts, &c. payable on Demand.]—For Stamp from
every piece of vellum, parchment, or paper, upon which 40s. to 5l.
any bill of exchange, draft, or order for the payment of 5s.
money *on demand*, shall be written, &c. where the sum
amounts to 40s. and does not exceed 5l. 5s. by 31 G. III.
c. 25. *three pence*; 37 G. III. *one penny*; and by 41 G. III.
c. 10. the additional sum of *two pence.* Total 6d.

When the sum shall be above 5l. 5s. and not exceeding From 5l. 5s.
30l. by 31 G. III. c. 25. *sixpence*; 37 G. III. c. 90. *two* to 30l.
pence; and by 41 G. III. c. 10. the additional sum of *four
pence.* Total, 1s.

When above 30l. and not exceeding 50l. by 31 G. III. From 30l.
c. 25. *nine pence*; 37 G. III. c. 90. *three pence*; and by to 50l.
41 G. III. c. 10. the additional sum of *sixpence.* Total,
1s. 6d.

Above 50l. and not exceeding 100l. by 31 G. III. c. 25. From 50l.
one shilling; 37 G. III. c. 90. *four pence*; and by 41 to 100l.
G. III. c. 10. the additional sum of *eight pence.* Total, 2s.

And where the sum shall exceed 100l. and shall not ex- From 100l.
ceed 200l. by 31 G. III. c. 25. *one shilling and sixpence*; to 200l.
37 G. III. c. 90. *sixpence*; and by 41 G. III. c. 10. the
additional sum of *one shilling.* Total, 3s.

Where the sum shall exceed 200l. by 41 G. III. c. 10. Above 200l.
the additional sum of *one shilling and four pence.* Total,
3s. 4d.

Any promissory note, or other note for the payment of Notes re-
money to the bearer *on demand*, which may be re-issuable issuable,
from time to time, after payment, at the place where it from 40s. to
was first issued, where the sum amounts to 40s: and shall 5l. 5s.
not exceed 5l. 5s. by 31 G. III. c. 25. *three pence*; 37
G. III. c. 90. *one penny*; and by 41 G. III. c. 10. *two
pence.* Total, 6d.

And where such sum shall exceed 5l. 5s. and not ex- From 5l. 5s.
ceed 30l. by 31 G. III. c. 25. *sixpence*; 37 G. III. c. 90. to 30l.

M 2　　　　　　　　　　　　　　　　　*two*

two pence; and by 41 *G. III. c.* 10, the additional fum of *four pence*. Total, 1s.

Above 30l. and not exceeding 50l. by 25 *G. III. c.* 25, *nine pence*; 37 *G. III. c.* 90, *three pence*; and by 41 *G. III. c.* 10, the additional fum of *fixpence*. Total, 1s. 6d.

Above 50l. and not exceeding 100l. 31 *G. III. c.* 25, *one fhilling*; 37 *G. III. c.* 90, *four pence*; and by 41 *G. III. c.* 10, the additional fum of *eight pence*. Total, 2s.

And where fuch fum fhall exceed 100l. and fha'll not exceed 200l. by 31 *G. III. c.* 25, *one fhilling and fixpence*; 37 *G. III. c.* 90, *fixpence*; and by 41 *G. III. c.* 10, the additional fum of *one fhilling* Total, 3s.

Where the promiffory note fhall be paid by the perfon by whom the fame fhall have been made or figned, and firft iffued, and at the place where the fame were firft iffued, the perfon fo paying the fame, notwithftanding fuch payment may at any time afterwards, and fo often as there fhall be occafion after every fuch payment thereof, but not otherwife, again iffue and negotiate fuch notes; and every fuch note is declared to be, *after payment*, but not otherwife, iffuable and negotiable. But if fuch notes fhall be paid by any other than the perfon making or figning the fame, or at any place other than the place of iffuing, fuch notes fhall be conftrued to be vacated and fatisfied, and fhall be no longer negotiable, but fatisfied; and if any perfon fhall again iffue any fuch note after payment by any perfon other than the perfon making the fame, or at any place other than the place of iffuing, or if any perfon named in fuch note for payment thereof, fhall after payment neglect or refufe to cancel the fame, fuch perfon fhall forfeit 20l. And if fuch note fhall not be cancelled, then, and as often as it fhall be again iffued, theie fhall be due, anfwered, and paid, the like duty as was firft charged on fuch note, to be payable by and charged on the perfon who fhall again iffue, and negotiate fuch note.

Not re-iffu-
able without
ftamping
them with
a p oper
ftamp.

But by 41 *G. III. c.* 10, *f.* 7. no note re-iffuable by any act or acts in force before the paffing of this act, fhall, from and after the 5th of June 1801, be again iffued after payment thereof, until it fhall be brought to the head office to be ftampt with a proper ftamp; and the commiffioners are required to caufe the fame to be ftampt on payment of the duty by this act impofed, on proof on oath before the faid commiffioners that the fame hath not been,

after

after any payment thereof, again iſſued ſince the 5th of *June* 1801, and that the ſame have not been laid aſide for the purpoſe of being cancelled, at any time before the paſſing of this act; and any ſuch promiſſory or other notes which ſhall be firſt iſſued, or negotiated after the ſaid 5th of June 1801, and which may be re-iſſued after any payment thereof, according to the regulations of the ſaid act again iſſued, being alſo firſt ſtampt with the proper ſtamp to denote the duty by this act impoſed, may be again iſſued from time to time in the manner allowed by the ſaid acts reſpectively; and all rules, regulations, duties, and penalties preſcribed or impoſed by the ſaid acts, or any of them, with reſpect to the ſtamping ſuch promiſſory or other notes, in order to iſſue the ſame from time to time, or with reſpect to the iſſuing or negotiating or cancelling ſuch notes after payment thereof, ſhall be applied and put in practice with reſpect to the ſecuring the duties by this act impoſed, according to the true intent and meaning of this act, as fully and effectually to all intents and purpoſes, as if the ſame had been ſeverally enacted in the body of this act.

For any promiſſory or other note, payable to the bearer *Paying to* on demand, which may be re-iſſued, after payment at the *bearer on* ſame or any other place than where firſt iſſued, where the *demand.* ſum ſhall amount to 40s. and not exceed 5l. 5s. by 31 *G. III. c.* 25, *ſixpence*; 37 *G. III. c.* 90. *two pence*; and by the 41 *G. III. c.* 10, *four pence.* Total, 1s.

Above 5l. 5s. and not exceeding 30l. by 31 *G. III. c.* 25, *one ſhilling*; 37 *G. III. c.* 90, *four pence*; and by the 41 *G III. c.* 10, the additional ſum of *eight pence.* Total, 2s.

[It is declared that theſe notes may, as often as occaſion ſhall require, be again iſſued by the perſon making the ſame, notwithſtanding ſuch notes have been paid by the perſon making the ſame, or any other perſon in purſuance of any appointment for the payment thereof.]

Bills and Notes payable after date.] For every bill of *Bills after* exchange, draft, or order, payable otherwiſe than on de- *date from* mand, or any promiſſory or other note payable otherwiſe *40s. to 30l.* than to the bearer on demand, where the ſum ſhall amount to 40s. and not exceed 30l. by 31 *G. III. c.* 25, *ſixpence*; 37 *G. III. c.* 90, *two pence*; and by 41 *G. III. c.* 10, the additional ſum of *four pence.* Total, 1s.

And

From 30l. to 50l.   And where fuch fum fhall exceed 30l. and not exceed 50l. by 31 G. III. c. 25, *nine pence*; 37 G. III. c. 90, *three pence*; and by 41 G. III. c. 10, *fixpence.* Total, 1s. 6d.

From 50l. to 100l.   Above 50l. and not exceeding 100l. by 31 G. III. c. 25, *one fhilling*; 37 G. 3. c. 90, *four pence*; and by 41 G. III. c. 10 *eight pence.* Total, 2s.

From 100l. to 200l.   Above 100l. and not exceeding 200l. by 31 G. III. c. 25, *one fhilling and fixpence*; 37 G. III. c. 90, *fixpence*; and by 41 G. III. c. 10, the additional fum of *one fhilling.* Total, 3s.

Exceeding 200l.   On any promiffory note, or note payable on demand or otherwife, where the fum expreffed therein, or made payable thereby, fhall exceed 200l. there fhall be charged, by 31 G. III. c. 25, *two fhillings*; 37 G. III. c. 90, *eight pence*; and by 41 G. III. c. 10, the additional fum of *one fhilling and four pence.* Total, 4s.

Which duties fhall be paid by the perfon making or figning fuch bill, &c.

Foreign bills.   *Foreign Bills of Exchange.*] Drawn in fets, according to the cuftom of merchants, where the fum fhall not exceed 100l. fhall be charged, by 31 G. III. c. 25, *fixpence*; 37 G. III. c. 90, *three pence*; and by the 41 G. III. c. 10, the additional fum of *four pence.* Total, 1s. 1d.—Where the fum fhall exceed 100l. and not 200l. 31 G. III. c. 25, *nine pence*; 37 G. III. c. 90, *three pence*; and by 41 G. III. c. 10, the additional fum of *fixpence.* Total, 1s. 6d.—And exceeding 200l. by 31 G. III. c. 25, *one fhilling*; 37 G. III. c. 90, *four pence*; and by 41 G. III. c. 10, the additional fum of *eight pence.* Total, 2s.—And every bill of each fet fo drawn is declared to be chargeable with the duty.

By the laft-mentioned act of 41 G. III. the commencement of the new duties, is from and after April 5, 1801.

Exemptions from thefe Duties.

1. Drafts, or orders, payable to bearer on demand, bearing date on or before the day on which they fhall be iffued, and at the place from which they fhall be drawn and iffued, and drawn upon any banker, or perfon acting as a banker, and refiding and tranfacting bufinefs as a banker within ten miles of the place where fuch draft or order fhall be actually drawn and iffued.

2. All

2. All notes and bills issued by the Bank of England, on condition of their paying into the Exchequer the annual sum of 12,000*l.* in half-yearly payments, on *October* 10, and *April* 5.

Regulations made by the 31 *G. III. c.* 25, *still in force.*

If any bill, &c. shall be written on paper not stampt, or stampt with a stamp of lower value than directed; then there shall be due and paid the full duty hereby chargeable; which shall be payable by all persons who shall draw or make, and utter and negociate such bills, &c. *f.* 6.

And, by the same statute, all persons who shall write or sign, or cause to be written or signed, or who shall accept *or pay*, or cause to be accepted or paid, any bill, &c. without being first stampt with a proper stamp, or upon which there shall not be some stamp resembling the same, shall forfeit 20*l. f.* 10.

And it is enacted in the 9th section of the same statute, that every promissory or other note, which shall be issued after payment under this act, shall notwithstanding be payable to the person holding the same; and such person may maintain an action thereupon.

And, by the 19th section, no bill, &c. shall be available in law or equity, unless stamped with the lawful stamp, and that it shall not be lawful for the commissioners to stamp any paper, &c. after any bill, &c. shall be written thereon, under any pretence whatever.

But, by the 37 *G. III. c.* 136, it shall be lawful for any person, who shall be the holder of any bill, note, draft, or order, made after *July* 20, 1797, which shall have a stamp of a different denomination from that which is required, if the same shall be of equal or superior value to the stamp required, to produce the same within the times herein after mentioned, to the head office, or such officer as the commissioners shall appoint; and the commissioners may direct the proper officer, upon payment of the duty, and such penalty as is after mentioned, over and above the duty, to stamp such bill, note, draft, or order, with the proper stamp, and to give a receipt for the duty and penalty, so paid, on the back of such bill, note, draft, or order.

If any such bill, note, draft, or order, shall be produced before the same shall be payable, the same shall be stamped on payment of the said duty, and the penalty of 40s. but if the same shall be payable before the production thereof to the commissioners, then the same shall not be stamped, unless on payment of the duty and 10*l.* penalty.

SMALL BILLS AND NOTES.

Duties on small notes. By the 39 *G. III. c.* 107, it is enacted, that from and after December 1, 1799, there shall be charged, assessed, and paid on bills of exchange and promissory notes for small sums, the several duties herein-after mentioned, that is to say—

On a pound and guinea note. For every bill of exchange, promissory note, or other note, draft, or order, whether payable on demand or otherwise, where the sum expressed therein shall be for one pound, and one pound and one shilling each, there shall be charged a stamp duty of *two pence.*

5s. note. And where the sum expressed therein shall be five shillings, as herein-after mentioned, there shall be charged a stamp duty of *one halfpenny.*

Notes re-issuable. For every promissory note or other note for the payment of money to the bearer on demand, payable only at the place where the same was first issued, and which may be re-issuable from time to time after payment at that place, where the sum expressed therein shall be for one pound, or one pound one shilling, there shall be charged a duty of *two pence.* And where the sum expressed therein shall be five shillings, there shall be a stamp duty of *one halfpenny.*

To the bearer on demand. For every promissory note or other note for the payment of money to the bearer on demand, payable at two or more different places, or at any place different from that where it shall have been originally issued, and which may be re-issued from time to time after payment at the same place, or any other place than where the same was first issued, where the sum expressed therein shall be for one pound, or one pound and one shilling, there shall be charged a stamp duty of *four pence.* And where the sum expressed therein, or made payable thereby, shall be 5*s.* a stamp duty of *one penny.* N. B. The 5*s.* notes are only issuable in Scotland.

The duty is payable by the person who gives the note.

Drafts on a banker. But nothing in this act shall extend to charge any draft or order for the payment of money on demand, upon any banker,

banker, or person acting as a banker, residing within ten miles of the place of abode of the drawer. And the Bank of England notes are exempted from the duties charged by this act on a composition of 4000*l.* and from all additional duties imposed since the act of 31 *G. III. c.* 25, on a composition of 8000*l.* payable half yearly.

No bill of exchange shall be re-issued; but notes payable on demand, on which a duty of *two pence,* or *one half penny,* is respectively imposed, paid by persons giving them at the places where first issued, may be re-issued; but if paid by any other persons or at any other place, in pursuance of appointment expressed therein, shall be cancelled; and if re-issued, or if not cancelled, the party to forfeit 20*l.* And such notes not cancelled, but again issued, shall pay the same as when first issued. **Bills of exchange not re-issuable.**

Notes which shall be stamped with the duty of four pence, and one penny, respectively, may be re-issued, though paid by other persons than by whom, and at other places than where first issued. And notes so re-issuable shall be the property of the persons holding them.

And whereas two acts passed in the 15th and 17th *G. III.* to restrain the negotiation of promissory notes under five pounds, made and negotiated in England, have been by several subsequent acts of the 37th, 38th and 39th of *G. III.* suspended until and upon the 5th of July 1799, so as the same relate to any notes, drafts, or undertakings made payable on demand to the bearer thereof: and whereas it is expedient further to suspend the said acts of the 15th and 17th years aforesaid, so far as the same relate to such notes which shall be made for sums of one pound and one shilling, and of one pound, each; be it further enacted, that the said recited acts of the 15th and 17th years aforesaid, so far as they relate to the making void of promissory notes, or other notes made payable on demand to the bearer thereof, for sums of one pound and one shilling, and of one pound, each, and also so far as the same restrain the publishing and negotiating of any such promissory notes, or other notes as aforesaid, shall, from and after the 5th of July 1799, be further suspended until and upon the 30th of November, 1802. **Negotiation of certain notes suspended.**

From July 5, 1799, the Bank of Scotland, and the Royal Bank of Scotland, the British Linen Company, the Carron Company, and all other banks and banking companies in Scotland, may issue notes payable to bearer on demand for **Bank of Scotland, &c. may issue small notes.**

N

5*s.* Sterling, as they have heretofore issued notes for 20*s.* and upwards. And such issue may continue till December 1, 1800, and to the end of the next session.

Provided that no bill of exchange, promissory note, bill, ticket, or other note in the nature of bank notes, shall, after the first of December, 1799, be issued in Scotland for any sums under five pounds Sterling, except for five shillings or one guinea, on penalty of 10*l.* But the banks or companies in Scotland may, on license, issue or re-issue notes for five shillings Sterling, and also one pound, and one guinea, drawn under the regulations mentioned in the act, unstamped, on giving security for the payment of the duties.

After December 1, 1799, no persons, except the Directors of the Bank or the Royal Bank of Scotland, or persons acting under them, are licensed to sign or issue any unstamped note.

Acts respecting stamp duties, not hereby altered, to extend to this act.

NOTARIES FEES OF OFFICE, AS REGULATED ON THE 1ST OF JULY, 1797.

AT a meeting of a considerable number of notaries of the city of London, held at the George and Vulture tavern, July 1, 1797, the following resolutions were agreed to, and since approved and confirmed by the Governor and Company of the Bank of England—

Within and without the walls. *First,* That after the 5th of July, 1797, the noting for all bills drawn upon, or addressed at the house of any person residing within the walls of the city of London, shall be charged one shilling and sixpence; and without the walls, and not exceeding the limits here-under specified, two shillings and sixpence.

Second, For all bills drawn upon, or addressed at the house of any person residing between Old or New Bond-street, Wimpole-street, New Cavendish-street, Upper Mary-bone-street, Howland-street, Lower Gower-street, lower end of Gray's-inn-lane (and not off the pavement), Clerkenwell Church, Old-street, Shoreditch Church, Brick-

Brick-lane, St. George's in the East, Execution-dock, Wapping, Dock-head, upper end of Bermondsey-street (as far as the church), end of Blackman-street, end of Great Surrey-street, Blackfriars-road (as far as the Circus), Cuper's Bridge, Bridge-street, Westminster, Arlington-street, Piccadilly, and the like distances, three shillings and sixpence; and off the pavement, one shilling and sixpence per mile additional.

Third, For protesting a bill drawn upon, or addressed at the house of any person residing within the ancient walls of the city of London (including the stamp-duty of four shillings, and exclusive of the charge of noting), six shillings and sixpence; and without the ancient walls of the city, including the like stamp duty, and exclusive of the said charge of noting, eight shillings, agreeable to the second article.

Fourth, That all *acts of honour* within the ancient walls of the said city, shall be charged the sum of one shilling and sixpence upon each bill; and for all acts of honour without the ancient walls of the said city, to be regulated agreeable to the charge of noting bills out of the city; and the like charge for any additional demand that may be made upon the said bill, or when the same is mentioned and inserted in the answer in the protest.

Fifth, For every *post demand and act thereof,* within the ancient walls of the said city, two shillings and sixpence; and without the walls of the said city, three shillings and sixpence (provided the same be only registered in the notary's books), and so in proportion according to the distance, to be regulated agreeable to the charge of noting bills.

Sixth, For every *copy of bill paid in part,* and a receipt at foot of *such copy,* two shillings; and so in proportion for every additional bill so copied, exclusive of the receipt stamp.

Seventh, For every *duplicate protest* of one bill (including four shillings for the duty), shall be charged seven shillings and sixpence; and so in like proportion of three shillings and sixpence (exclusive of the duty) for every additional bill.

Eighth, For every folio of *ninety words,* translated from the French, Dutch, or Flemish, into English, shall be charged one shilling and sixpence; and from English into French, Dutch or Flemish, two shillings for each such folio; and from Italian, Spanish, Portugueze, German,

Danish, and Swedish, one shilling and nine pence per folio of ninety words; and from Latin two shillings and sixpence per folio; and for attesting the same to be a true translation, if necessary, seven shillings and sixpence, exclusive of fees and stamps.

Ninth, That all *attestations to letters of attorney,* affidavits, &c. at the request of any gentleman in the law, shall be charged seven shillings and sixpence, exclusive of fees, stamps, and attendance.

Tenth, For every *city seal,* one guinea for one deponent, exclusive of attendance, and exemplification; and if more than one deponent, ten shillings and sixpence for each additional affidavit.

Eleventh, For all *notarial copies* shall be charged sixpence per folio of seventy-two words, exclusive of attestation, stamps, &c. *Chitty's Tr. 952.*

APPENDIX.

By 44 G. III. c. 98. a new regulation respecting notes, and bills of exchange, took place.

By this act, a promissory note, for the payment of money to bearer on demand (which may, within three years, but not at a later period, be re-issued) where the sum shall not exceed one pound and one shilling

	£.	s.	d.
...shilling	0	0	3
Exceeding 1 *l.* 1 *s.* and not 2 *l.* 2 *s.*	0	0	6
Exceeding 2 *l.* 2 *s.* and not 5 *l.* 5 *s.*	0	0	9
Exceeding 5 *l.* 5 *s.* and not 20 *l.*	0	1	0

Promissory note by the bank of Scotland, or royal bank of Scotland, or the British linen company, payable to bearer on demand, which may within three years be re-issued where the sum amounts to and shall not exceed one hundred pounds — 0 5 0

Bill of exchange, or promissory or other note, payable to the bearer on demand, for forty shillings, and not exceeding 5 *l.* 5 *s.* — 0 0 8

———————— otherwise than to the bearer on demand, where the sum shall amount to forty shillings, and shall not exceed 5 *l.* 5 *s.* — 0 1 0

Bill of exchange, or promissory or other note, for the payment of money, where the sum shall exceed 5 *l.* 5 *s.* and not 30 *l.* — 0 1 6

Exceeding 30 *l.* and not 50 *l.*	0	2	0
Exceeding 50 *l.* and not 100 *l.*	0	3	0
Exceeding 100 *l.* and not 200 *l.*	0	4	0
Exceeding 200 *l.* and not 500 *l.*	0	5	0
Exceeding 500 *l.* and not 1,000 *l.*	0	7	6
Exceeding 1,000 *l.*	0	10	0

Foreign bills of exchange drawn in sets, not exceeding one hundred pounds, for each bill in each set — 0 1 0

Exceeding 100 *l.* and not 200 *l.*	0	2	0
Exceeding 200 *l.* and not 500 *l.*	0	3	0
Exceeding 500 *l.* and not 1,000 *l.*	0	4	0
Exceeding 1,000 *l.*	0	5	0

By the same statute, the following exemptions are allowed, *viz.*

Bills of exchange, promissory, and other notes and bills, issued by the bank of England, are exempted, on condition of their paying annually 32,000 *l.*

Draft

Drafts on a banker for the payment of money, if within ten miles of the place at which such draft shall be given, shall also be exempted.

No note payable to bearer on demand, which shall bear date before or on October 10th, 1804, shall be reissued after October 10th, 1805, but shall be cancelled on penalty of 20l. f. 21.

INDEX.

A.

ACCEPTANCE, what, 13. Is an engagement to pay, id. May be written or verbal, id. What amounts to an, 14. What does not amount to an, 15. Implied, id. Promise to, id. May differ from the tenor of the bill, 16. Conditional, id. For the honour of the drawer, 17.

Acceptance to a bill payable after sight must be dated, 14. What is not an, 69.

Acceptance of a forged bill, 17.

Accommodation bill may be proved, 56.

Act of bankruptcy, paying after, 55.

Actions, separate, against the parties, 71.

Administrators must discharge bonds before bills of exchange, 9.

Agents may be empowered to draw, accept, and indorse bills, 53.

Altering a bill of exchange, 8. In what case it requires a new stamp, id.

Assigning a bill knowing it to be of no value, 26.

B.

Bank of England may issue notes, 43. Which are to many purposes considered as money, id. And a tender in payment, 44. Exempted from stamp duty, 45.

Bankruptcy, in, bills and notes devolve upon the assignees, 31. Bankrupt's property vests in the assignees, 54. Bill drawn before, and accepted after, 56. Respecting petitioning creditor, 59. Debt under a commission cannot be proved twice, 60. Where an indorser has not proved before payment, id.

Barter, prior to bills of exchange, 1.

Bearer, notes payable to, on demand, 46.

Bill not to be protested till the day after it becomes due, though a contrary custom still prevails, 38, 39.

Bill of exchange, foreign, 9. Inland, 10. Set of, what, id. Condition to be inserted in each, id.

Bills of exchange, origin of, 1. In use among the Romans and Jews, 2. When generally adopted, 3. Of the parties to, id. Description of, id. Must be in writing, 4. When upon contingency, or conditional, 5. Must be to pay money only, 6. Are entitled to three days grace, 7. Altering of, 8. Not negotiable after paid, 27. Holder of, may sue all parties, 32. Who may draw and negotiate, 52.

Bills of exchange, and notes, in some respects the same, 5. Are governed by calendar months, 11.

Bills payable at sight, different from those payable on demand, 8.

Bolland, executed for signing a fictitious name upon a bill of exchange, 30.

Blank paper, signing name on, 9. Indorsement on, 25. Are frequent, id.

C.

Calendar, not lunar months, are applied to bills of exchange, 11.

Chil

field's

FINIS.

Printed by W. Stratford, Crown-Court, Temple-Bar.

Milton Keynes UK
Ingram Content Group UK Ltd.
UKHW022105150124
436101UK00005B/109